CW01514050

POTS, BUTT

and many other things

by

Alan Ashpool

In this book the Author describes how he gave up the 'Day Job' in the Home Office to move to Dorset to open a Pottery and to spend more time photographing butterflies. He also describes the many other facets of country life that he encountered along the way in mini-chapters which ignore the actual timescale involved.

For Doreen

*Without her help I would never have
moved to Dorset or written this book*

ISBN Number 0-9552518-0-X   ISBN 13 digit 978-0-9552518-0-1

First published April 2006 by Alan Ashpool,
Trumps In Cottage, Whitchurch Canonicorum,
Bridport, Dorset, DT6 6RH.

Printed and bound in Great Britain
by Creeds the Printers
Broadoak, Bridport, Dorset, DT6 5NL, UK.

Contents

Appendices

A London Exhibition Poster

1. LIFE BEFORE THE MOVE

My life before the move was tiring and often stressful. Most days I would have to commute to my office in Victoria in an overcrowded train and, after hours in a busy office, repeat the experience in the evening. The highlights were making pottery and spending my holidays in Dorset.

I had become interested in making pottery in my early twenties when I was taught by the famous potter Heber Matthews and the pots that I made were sold by various London Stores and in group exhibitions. Holidays in Dorset with my wife Doreen were either in North Dorset near Blandford or in the west of the county at Chideock and from these bases we were able to explore most parts of this wonderful county. Doreen had been a librarian with a strong interest in Thomas Hardy and was able to introduce me to many of the places which were brought to life in his novels. There I was also able to see and photograph a number of butterflies, a lifelong passion with me, that could not be seen in and around London. Doreen and I often talked about how wonderful it would be if we could buy a house in Dorset and perhaps live there on a permanent basis. We daydreamed about this and watched television programmes which fed these dreams such as Jack Hargreaves 'A Life In The Country' and the film 'Far From The Madding Crowd'. There seemed however, no possible way we could do this. I would have had to work another seven years before I could draw my Civil Service pension and there was a large mortgage to pay off. We also felt that we should provide Mark, our teen-age son, with a home until he was fully able to fend for himself.

Suddenly things changed! Mark died in a tragic motorbike accident. There no longer seemed the need to live in London. At the same time local property prices rose at a much faster rate than in the rest of the country which meant in theory we could pay off our mortgage, buy a property in Dorset and have enough money over to exist until my pension became payable. We also felt that we might possibly supplement the income generated by this money by selling pottery and providing Bed and Breakfast accommodation. So our London house was put on the market and we made plans to find a suitable property in Dorset.

Some London Pots

2. HOUSE HUNTING

Of the two areas of Dorset where our holidays were spent we felt that Chideock would be the best place in which to search for our new home. It was nearer the sea which meant that there would probably be more tourists about to buy my pottery or stay with us for Bed and Breakfast. The first thing we did was to arrange for a weekly local newspaper to be sent to us. This contained several pages of details of properties for sale we were interested in and we decided that we would restrict our search to an area within 10 kilometres of the market town of Bridport. This encompassed Chideock and a number of other interesting villages.

The first priority was to find a property that we felt we could afford. Next priority was whether it had a workshop that could be used as a pottery and that it had sufficient bedrooms for providing bed and breakfast. Then, as I didn't drive, it had to have a good public transport service. Having decided which properties we would like to see, Doreen would phone on the Friday morning to make arrangements to view them on the Saturday. She would then drive us down to Dorset in our rusty Renault 4 on Friday afternoon. Our base was an old thatched inn called the Ilchester Arms in the village of Symondsbury which was just outside Bridport. We were familiar with this pub, and the tenants, having lunched there on numerous occasions when on holiday. We thought it would be a good place to stay for bed and breakfast but hadn't taken into account that it might be noisy at the weekend with skittle and darts matches going on. And noisy it was! Our bedroom was just over the main bar and every noise was amplified by a cavernous chimney which extended through the whole building. We didn't get much sleep and would stagger down to an enormous full English breakfast, which we struggled to finish because we didn't want to offend our hosts. On most mornings we couldn't finish and a large proportion had to be spirited away in a paper napkin! This scenario was to be repeated for several weekends. On each occasion we would view five or six properties on average and each time found none that were suitable for our purpose. Doreen would then drive us back to London on the Sunday filled with disappointment. On the last weekend trip we had lunch at The Bull, an old coaching inn in Bridport. When lunch was finished Doreen casually looked in the window of an Estate Agent close-by. There she saw details of an old cottage in the village of Whitchurch Canonicorum which caught her eye and, even though the selling price was above our upper limit, immediately made arrangements to see it.

The Ilchester Arms

3. TRUMPS IN COTTAGE

It was everything that I did not want. Firstly it was a Listed Building more than 400 years old which meant that it would be difficult to make any alterations to it! Secondly it was thatched which meant high insurance and repair costs! Thirdly it was in a village about 8 kilometres from Bridport which only had one bus a week and above all the selling price was quite a lot above our upper limit. The vendors, who I shall call Mr and Mrs X, were also in the middle of a messy divorce so we didn't know who we exactly had to deal with. Doreen loved it however, and it did have some outbuildings that might be suitable for a pottery, so we decided to have an independent survey on it.

The report of the survey added further to some of my anxieties. The surveyor basically said that about £20,000 would have to be spent on the property to get it into an inhabitable condition. This was the amount we had planned to keep to one side to cover our living expenses until I could draw my Civil Service pension. The survey said, amongst other things, that all the walls and ground floors of the cottage would have to be made damp proof, that it would have to be rewired, that it would need a new drainage system, that several of the window frames would have to be replaced and that some of the thatch and its supports would soon need attention. We sent a copy of the survey to Mr X who, although he was living away from the cottage, we thought we would be most happy to deal with. After he had studied it he invited us down so that we could have a much more detailed look at the cottage. We arrived there on a very cold frosty February morning after yet another night and breakfast at the Ilchester Arms. Mr X took me around the property to go over the points raised in the survey. All the time he was trying to convince me that the surveyor had got it wrong. Whilst he was able to provide evidence that the premises had recently been rewired he couldn't steer me away from what seemed to me the main problems namely the state of the drainage and the roof. When he lifted the cover of the septic tank inspection chamber it was flooded, which suggested that there was a serious blockage in the system. In the roof space all that seemed to be holding up the thatch were a number of branches from old apple trees and these were riddled with woodworm. Mr X suggested that the trouble in the septic tank could be cured by asking a couple of the local lads to dig a new soak-away. As for the roof he thought that the local thatcher could put some new branches of apple trees in the roof space which would keep it going for a few more years! I was not very happy with these suggestions and my basic instinct was to cut and run! Doreen still loved the cottage however, so we decided to go back to the surveyors to see whether there were any cheaper options to the repairs that they had suggested. They replied that their suggestions related to what had to be done in order to get the property into a pristine condition. They added that it would be possible to live in it in its present condition for a number of years without too much discomfort. In addition I learnt from a local thatcher that apple tree branches were often used as rafters in older thatched cottages. In the light of these revelations we decided to go ahead with the purchase. By this time our house in London had been sold and we thought that very shortly we would be the proud owners of Trumps In. There were some unforeseen difficulties in agreeing a completion date and we had to wait whilst they were being resolved. This took a couple of weeks of hair raising suspense but finally the deal went ahead. I tendered my resignation from the Civil Service and we prepared for the move.

Trumps In Cottage

4. THE MOVE

One of the problems to be overcome by the removal people would be that they couldn't take a lot of the bedroom furniture up the stairs in the cottage. It would have to be lifted up through a trapdoor in the main living room. For this reason we thought that we should use the same removers as Mrs X who would be familiar with this problem. This was a family firm from Axminster which is about 12 kilometres from the cottage. They regularly made removal trips to London and we were able to arrange for them to move us to Dorset. It was agreed that they would move Mrs X on one day and move us on the next. All went well with moving Mrs X to her new accommodation but things went rapidly wrong with the arrangements to move us. The removal men were due to arrive at the London house at 8am and move us out by 10am.The purchasers of our old house would then be able to move in as soon as they wished after we were packed up and away. However nobody turned up at 8am and we received a phone call from the removal firm in Axminster to say that they had lost contact with the men who were booked to move us out and they said that they would contact us as soon as they had more information. Fortunately the people who were due to move in were vacating a house just a few blocks away and I was able to walk round to them and explain our predicament. They were very understanding and said that they would get their removers to pack up their belonging and park outside our old house until after our removers arrived. At about 10.30 their removal van turned up, but we still didn't have any further information from our people. Two hours later we received a call to say that our removal van was on its way and should be with us before 2pm. The incoming family seemed happy with this and their removers decided to have a game of football in the street to fill in the time. Unfortunately the ball went into the garden of the people next door and their large dog went for them. Things went from bad to worse one of the removers kicked the dog and its owner appeared brandishing a shotgun. Feathers were ruffled all round and it took a lot of diplomacy to calm things down before the police became involved.

Things did calm down but there was still no sign of our removal van. Finally at about 4pm it did turn up, was quickly packed and set off for Dorset. We followed on in our trusty Renault 4 which was packed to the gunnels with things we thought might be needed if the removal van got delayed and couldn't unpack until the following morning. Our dog and two cats were also crammed in on the back seat. To gain access to our new house we had arranged with Mrs X that she would leave the key with the lady living next door. By setting off so late we wondered whether the neighbour would stay up until we arrived. After several stops to feed and water our animals we finally reached the Dorchester bypass at about 10pm. This meant that we should reach the cottage by eleven. As we stopped once more for the animals, we were passed by a familiar looking removal van. It was ours and we assumed that it would be at the cottage to meet us when we arrived but his was not to be. There was no sign of it when we finally arrived at Trumps In but luckily our new neighbours were still up however and gave us the keys. As it seemed that our furniture would not arrive until the next morning they kindly offered us a bed for the night. We thought we would have a word with the removers first and they said that they would unload a double mattress and some bedding from the van, and get it to us within half an hour. So we took the key and let ourselves in to our new home. It seemed very shabby with no furniture in the rooms and for a moment we wondered whether we had done the right thing. This mood lifted however when our bedding arrived and we started to make ourselves at home. It lifted further when we saw a hedgehog in the garden caught in the light of our bare windows.

We had made the move to Dorset and were living in the country!

5. SETTLING IN

The removers came and unloaded the rest of our worldly possessions the next morning. One of our first priorities was to buy some carpeting for the rooms on the ground floor of the cottage and for the stairs and landings. It had originally been agreed with Mrs X that all the carpets would be left in situ and so we had made a similar arrangement with the purchasers of our London house. Mr X had different ideas however, and so we needed to get some new carpets installed before we finally decided where our furniture could go. The purchasing and professional fitting of carpets had not been allowed for in our budget, so we went to see a local 'Carpet Man' and purchased a number of remnants which we could cut down to size. These were delivered on the top of a small saloon car and our new neighbour Chas helped us unload them. Then he helped me lay some of them.

Chas helped us in many other ways. He was locally born and bred and, until he retired shortly before we arrived, had been the village postman. Consequently he knew everyone and where they lived. Also he was deeply involved in the local church, was a regular at the local pub, belonged to the local Flower Show and Village Hall Committees. We couldn't have had a better neighbour! We were quickly introduced by him to so many people. Chas's wife Beryl was also very helpful. She had provided bed and breakfast accommodation in her cottage for many years and was able to provide a lot of advice on the subject. She was also able to let us know about the local provision of milk, bread, eggs, fish, meat and general groceries. Shortly after we had moved in, we were visited by the local Vicar who warmly welcomed us to the area. Two ladies from the WI also called and invited Doreen to come to their next meeting. Both of us felt how lucky we were to have moved to such a friendly place, and to have got to know so many people so soon after our arrival. Within three weeks we were regarded as regulars in the local pub, had been asked to serve ice- creams at the village flower show and became involved in the village hall.

The Village Hall

6. SETTING UP THE POTTERY

In order of priority setting up the pottery came very near the top of the list. With the exception of a kiln most of the equipment and materials from my old studio came down to Dorset with the rest of our goods and chattels. I didn't take the kiln because it was old, small, heavy and used a lot of electricity. One of my first tasks after moving in was to order a larger electric kiln which employed ceramic fibre for its insulation. This meant that it would use much less electricity to reach the temperature I required, that it would cool down more quickly and be much lighter to move. The next task was to get the local electricity suppliers to put in an electrical supply to the old workshops in the garden which I had decided to use as the pottery. As there was no central heating in the cottage we combined this with the installation of a number of night storage heaters. This enabled us to switch to the economy 7 electricity supply tariff and heat the kiln by using very cheap power overnight when its load was highest.

The garden buildings consisted of a very old and very small barn to which a wooden extension had been added by a recent tenant. Both where in a fairly dilapidated state so, while I was waiting for the new kiln to arrive, I set to fixing leaks, painting walls, preserving wood, putting up shelves and installing strip lights. When this had been done I started moving in some of my equipment and materials which had been unloaded and stored in the garage that is attached to Trumps In. Good old Chas next door helped me with some of the heavier items. He helped me again a few days later when the new kiln was delivered.

Once the workshop was laid out and the power was on I was able to decide on what other materials I would need in order to start work. Before the move I thought about what kind of pottery I would have to create in order to make a living. Previously I had only made individual one off pots which I sold mainly through exhibitions and specialist stores. In Dorset I felt that a lot of my work would have to be sold through craft fairs and at village events. To this end I used the potters wheel to make a large number small bowls, jugs, vases and mugs which I intended to cover with a number of shiny coloured glazes. At the same time I experimented with making items such as small lidded pots and house numbers using slip casting techniques. I hadn't had much previous experience with this method and it took some time designing and making the necessary moulds with potters plaster. Even more time was spent developing the clay slip that I could use. Manufacturers of clay bodies would usually give a recipe for making casting slip with a particular clay but it didn't always work. My first attempts resulted in warped thin walled pots, lids that didn't fit, cracks and different sized pieces from identical moulds.

Gradually I solved these problems and built up a stock of perfect casts ready to be fired in the new kiln. One of the first pieces I fired was an oval ceramic plaque which had the word 'Pottery' inscribed on it. It came out perfectly and I proudly put it up on the door of the workshop. The pottery was open for business!

7. THE VILLAGE

Whitchurch Canonicorum is situated in the valley of the Char river, in the beautiful Marshwood Vale which encompasses a number of villages in West Dorset and is surrounded by several hills. Its long name arose from the fact that the tithes were divided between the canons of Salisbury and Wells. The major lane through the village starts at the A35 at Morecombelake and then passes through Ryall before it enters Whitchurch at Trumps In Cottage. It then twists and turns for a couple of kilometres until it reaches Berne Lane and returns to the A35. There are a number of other lanes leading off from this main thoroughfare most of them have banks, hedges, and verges which in spring and summer have a good display of wild flowers which in turn attract numerous bees and butterflies. The houses in the village are a mix of old thatched cottages, detached Edwardian villas, pre and post war bungalows and 'chalets' and also a number of small farms. Earlier there had been many more old thatched dwellings but in the early 1900s a number of them were burnt down by a local arsonist. Most of the Edwardian buildings bear the date 1904 which suggests that they were built on the site of some of those burnt -out cottages. A number of the dwellings are situated around the church. Others are close to the Village Hall which is at the Berne Lane end of the village and to the Five Bells Inn which is situated at the other end. The present Five Bells was built in 1904 on the site of a very old thatched pub which had also fallen a victim to the arsonist mentioned above. When we arrived the village had a Post Office and small shop in addition to the pub and village hall but sadly these no longer exist.

This has happened in many other rural areas and often the local pub has also closed.

Social life in the village often revolves around the church, the village hall and the pub but there are other social gatherings such as the annual flower show and the Gymkhana. In the past the church played the most important social and historical roles in the life of the area. The parish church of St. Candida and Holy Cross is really the jewel of the village. It was built in Norman times but it is believed that an earlier Saxon one existed on the site. It

The Parish Church of St. Candida

is the only parish church in England to have what is thought to be the actual relic of a saint. The bones of a woman who may have been St. Wite are in a sealed casket built into the wall of the north transept. For centuries pilgrims came to put their crippled limbs into the three apertures built into the tomb in the hope of being healed. Even today many troubled people leave pleas to be helped at the shrine.

The Shrine of St. Wite

The building which is now the village hall was previously the village school. It was built in 1840 and served the village and surrounding district until it closed towards the end of the 1960s. In 1970 a committee was set up to buy the building so that it could be used as a village hall. After a lot of hard work to raise the funds for it the hall was officially opened in November 1971. In addition to events organised by the Village Hall Committee to raise money for maintenance it is used for many other functions e.g. WI meetings, playgroup, charity events, harvest suppers and young farmers' meetings. Now the village hall and the pub possibly play as big a role in the social life of the village as the church.

8. FIRST BUTTERFLIES

When we came to Dorset on holiday photographing butterflies was a very hit and miss affair. I would go on random walks along lanes or footpaths and take pot-shots with my camera of any butterfly that settled close by. Many attempts resulted in a blurred picture, or in some cases no picture at all, as the subject suddenly took off. Shortly after the move however I found a book in the local library entitled 'Butterflies of Dorset'. It contained distribution maps, times on the wing and flight patterns of all the butterfly species that might be seen in the county. It was so detailed that I went and ordered a copy right away from a bookshop in Bridport. It proved invaluable as it enabled me to plan visits to particular habitats to photograph particular species of butterfly at the right times. Once I had read about the flight patterns of a particular species, and how they displayed their wings when at rest, I was able devise a strategy to photograph that species more successfully.

The first butterflies I saw after the move were typical species of late summer such as Gatekeepers, Walls, Speckled Woods, Marbled Whites, Small Coppers. and Holly Blues There were also the aristocrats such as Red Admirals, Small Tortoiseshells, Peacocks and the occasional Painted Lady all being attracted to the buddleia and valerian flowers which were in blossom. I had seen all these species before but not in such numbers. What I had never seen before was a butterfly taking nectar from sea campion flowers at West Bexington on the West Bay end of Chesil Beach. At first Ithought it was the very rare Pale Clouded Yellow or possibly Berger's Clouded Yellow. It just seemed too good to be true! The excitement was so overpowering that I was unable to focus my camera and the creature flew away! When I got home however and looked in my new butterfly book I leant that it was a white form of the female Clouded Yellow called *helice*. The Clouded Yellow itself is not very common in most years but its numbers far outstrip those of the species I thought I had seen. This was to be the first of many mis-identifications that I was to make during my life in Dorset. Not only of butterflies but of birds and wild flowers as well. Fortunately there were to be many real firsts .

In the spring and summer following our move I saw for the first time butterflies such as the Green Hairstreak, the Small Pearl- bordered Fritillary, the Grayling, the Dingy Skipper, the Silver-studded Blue, the Dark Green Fritillary and the White Admiral. Not all of these were spotted in the Marshwood Vale. Some were seen in the stone quarries on the Isle of Portland and others in North Dorset. There was also a sighting of that special Dorset butterfly the Lulworth Skipper. This was later to play a special place in my life when it was depicted on a large ceramic mural I was involved in making. Dorset is such a wonderful place for butterflies and has been an inspiration for artists such as Gordon Beningfield. I was able to get an insight into this inspiration over the years I spent photographing these wonderful creatures.

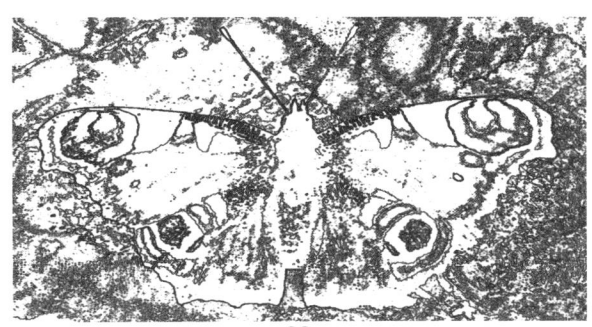

9. BED AND BREAKFAST

Whenever we had moved to a new house in the past we have been besieged by visitors before we had a real chance to get straight. This move was no exception! Even more so! First there were old work colleagues eager to see how we were faring after giving up a good job and accommodation in London. Then there were friends from my evening classes. Also there were people from Doreen's job in the library and from her classes for the deaf. On top of this many of our real old friends decided that they would like to spend a holiday in the country. With this rush of visitors taking up our time and accommodation, there was little opportunity for us to start our bed and breakfast business for many months after our arrival. Letting bed and breakfast accommodation was to have been a source of useful income and we hadn't planned for feeding and accommodating so many friends and colleagues.

Eventually things did get better. By the time the next tourist season came around we were able to start advertising, by word of mouth, that we could provide a double bed and a single bed accommodation on a bed and breakfast basis. Our first approach was to contact larger local established accommodation providers such as farm complexes and hotels saying that we could help out if, for example, they were full or had double-booked. This resulted in quite a few bookings. Such an approach had the added advantage that quite a lot of preliminary vetting of the guests had already been carried out and we could feel that they were genuine. As time went on however we began to build up a guest list of our own with people coming back year after year. We also got a lot of bookings from our local pub. This had a large camping site which was suitable for younger people and their children but not for older members of the family. They preferred a proper bed and as our cottage was just opposite they often stayed with us. The pub also ran a number of sporting events for groups such as cricketers and motorcyclists where they provided all the meals but we provided the sleeping arrangements. This meant that some weekends there were people sleeping in all of our bedrooms and we had a makeshift bed downstairs. At other times we put up families with several children which again meant more nights for us downstairs. Then there were problem people. These included a wife who couldn't get up in the morning because she had a hangover and a family with a disruptive autistic child. Mostly however, guests came down for breakfast at a reasonable time and went on their way.

Doreen quite enjoyed having people staying and chatted away quite happily with them. For my part I felt uneasy about having strangers in the house. If possible I would rise early and take the dogs for a walk that would last until I thought that breakfast was over and our guests had left. Having said that the extra income that providing bed and breakfast brought in was, in the early days crucial to our survival. Later when we had other sources of income we were able to scale down this operation. Many of our regulars however continued to stay with us. Once we had got to know them they ceased to be strangers and I felt more at ease when they were staying with us.

10. THE FIVE BELLS

Until we saw the local plans attached to the exchange contract we had not realised that there was a village pub just a few hundred yards down the road from Trumps In Cottage. One of the joys of coming to Dorset on holiday was eating and drinking in country pubs so we were delighted to have one within walking distance of our new cottage. The Five Bells was at that time a typical friendly local with an easy atmosphere which could be enjoyed by both locals and tourists alike. There were two rooms leading off from the entrance hall. The room on the right contained the one small bar and was basically furnished with a large oak settle plus a few old tables and chairs. On the left was a family room also basically furnished with a jumble of old tables and chairs. The bar stocked a couple of local real ales and a draught cider together with a small assortment of bottled drinks, wines and spirits. Simple bar food was served in both rooms but there wasn't much of a choice. It is a tied house belonging to Palmers Brewery in Bridport who also own many of the other pubs in the area. A number of different publicans have taken over the tenancy since we came to the village each one running it in their own way.

The most vibrant times were, in my opinion, when it was run by four people who took the tenancy over on a shared basis about a year after we arrived in the village. They arranged many exciting events to raise funds for charity, held good parties and provided a much wider range of food. The charity events were often to raise funds for Great Ormand Street Hospital for Sick Children (GOSH) with which they had connections. There would be a Slave

Auction where people would undertake a certain task for the highest bidder. There were markets for all kinds of things and services including a Fortune Telling Tent. There was a Hot Air Balloon which was tethered by a hundred-foot rope. There were stocks were anyone making a large enough donation to GOSH could pour a bucket of slurry over a volunteer sat in them. There were Charity Meals and Cream Teas where all profits went to GOSH. The list is endless. At New Year they held some very good fancy dress parties. They also put on a very lavish firework display and bonfire on Guy Fawkes night. The food that they produced matched the splendid variety of their charity events. There were ploughmens, salads, burghers and sandwiches. If you didn't like the choice of fillings for the later, you were invited to invent your own. There were such things as egg and chips, venison sausages, steak and kidney pie, chilli con carne, moussaka, lasagne, shepherds pie, various curries and steaks. Vegetarians were offered a vegetable lasagne, a nut roast and vegetable curry. In season they offered whole spider crabs with nutcrackers and salad. Soups on the menu included rat soup but it was pointed out that they only used organically raised vegetarian rats. Omelettes included mushroom, ham, cheese, tuna, hedgehog, whale and anything else.

This was also a good time for me as the village potter. The new tenants ordered a large number of different sized flat bottom stoneware dishes to serve and freeze their wide selection of dishes. They also ordered a number of posy pots which they filled with wild flowers to adorn an increased number of dinning tables. Both locals and regular visitors ordered stoneware pint beer mugs from me which I decorated and glazed to individual requirements. At one time there were more than twenty hanging up in the bar.

Sadly none remain now perhaps because they held a generous pint which later landlords could not subsidise. However, they did help to give the bar an air of individuality. There were many other interesting touches introduced by these four. For example they provided two or three boxes of different snuffs on the bar which could be sampled by customers. Locals could also leave their own snuffs above the bar to be shared and tried out. Fresh fish and crustaceans caught at West Bay by one of the four would be sold to locals at less than wholesale rates.

They were memorable days!

The Five Bells Sign

11. BREAKING A WRIST

Early in our first winter in Dorset we took some friends to a pub in Seatown which is on the coast and a popular tourist attraction. After a good lunch our friends thought they would like to see the view from the top of nearby Golden Cap, the highest hill on the south coast, so we set off up the footpath that led to the summit. The path was very muddy and we had some trouble negotiating it going up. Coming down was even trickier. All of us slipped over at some point but Doreen fell on her wrist and when we finally got back to the pub, it was clear that she had broken it so one of our friends drove her to the nearest A and E hospital in Weymouth some thirty kilometres to the East. They confirmed the fracture, plastered her up and said that she couldn't drive for at least eight weeks. This meant that we would have to rely on public transport. The weekly village bus was clearly not sufficient for either our shopping requirements or our social life. So two or three times a week we hiked the two kilometres to the A35 for the regular hourly bus to Bridport. Although the walk to the bus stop was uphill all the way it meant that when we returned laden with shopping we would have an easy journey down.

News of Doreen's broken arm spread quickly by 'bush telegraph'. For example shortly after the accident I took the dog for a walk to explore a coppice a few kilometres from the cottage. There I got into conversation with the man who owned it. To my surprise one of the first things he said was "I hear that your wife has broken her wrist." He then offered me a few swigs of cider from a large pottery loving cup in commiseration. Vegetables and bunches of flowers were left on our doorstep. Strangers came up and spoke to us to ask whether we needed any help or would like a lift to the shops. This was all very new to us coming from London where no strangers would enquire how you were or even pass the time of day.

One of the drawbacks to using the buses on the A 35 was that if we came back after dark we had to walk home down the very dark lanes. There were no street lights and we couldn't see very well by torchlight. Local villagers seemed well adjusted to the lack of light and would recognise us in complete darkness and say hello. It was quite a time before our night vision got as keen as theirs. An up side to this darkness was that on clear nights it was possible to see the stars in all their glory. The street lighting in London had obscured them from us for so long.

Doreen's plaster eventually came off. The car came out of its cocoon and then things returned to normal.

View of Golden Cap

12. SELLING POTS

Jugs and Mugs

Once the car could be used again, I turned my mind to finding outlets for my pots. Since setting up the pottery I had amassed a large number of thrown domestic ware, slip caste dishes and house numbers which I needed to sell to make ends meet. As mentioned earlier, the Five Bells bought a lot of pots from me and provided an outlet for beer mugs, but I realised that I would have to go further a field to keep my stock turning over. A regular at the pub suggested that he could sell a lot of my work in his gallery at West Bay but he could only do this on a sale or return basis. Before coming to Dorset I had tried to avoid this type of arrangement because it tied up a lot of stock, it restricted the cash flow and you could lose pots through shoplifting or even the gallery owner going bust.

Apparently however, most of the galleries in the county seemed to operate on this basis, and so reluctantly I had to agree to it.

The only other way that I could see to raise money from my pots was to sell directly to the public or at Art Exhibitions. Craft Fairs seemed one way of selling directly but had the disadvantage that pots had to be packed, taken to a venue by car, unpacked, set out and then re-packed at the end of the day to be taken home. And the stalls at Craft Fairs had to be paid for and stewarded. Another way of selling directly was to have a showroom at the pottery but we would had to have had listed building planning permission to do this and early soundings with the District Council suggested that this would be refused. Art Exhibitions usually entailed an entrance fee together with a commission levied on any Sales.

None of the above mentioned sale methods seemed sufficient on their own to give us a regular income, so we decided that all of them should be adopted. Several galleries and craft shops in Dorset and Devon who had been told about my work by friends contacted us. Samples of my pots were shown to them and several agreed to stock them. Most craft shows were one off affairs run by various charities or Village Halls. These were often poorly organised and sometimes we spent a whole day where our sales didn't cover the hire cost of the table. We soon learnt to avoid these. A regular series however were held in the summer at Bridport Arts Centre which attracted a lot of visitors. Doreen would often go to these on her own if I had work to finish in the pottery and these proved to be quite lucrative. On some days she would sell well over £100 worth of work. People would often place orders for particular pots and craft shop proprietors would arrange visits to the pottery to buy off the shelf.

The only Art Exhibition that I regularly supported in the early days was that run each year in our Village Hall. This always had a good display of paintings by local artists together with a range of crafts. Sales were good and the commission charged was only 15%. We also sold pottery at the Church Fete and the Village Flower Show on a similar commission basis. After two or three years of selling in this way I managed to get some regular sales on a cash basis. Moores Biscuit Factory in nearby Morcombelake ordered and sold a large number of my ceramic house numbers each year in their shop gallery, and the famous Broadwindsor Craft Centre placed regular cash orders for a range of my domestic ware. All this kept the wolf from the door until I started to draw my Civil Service pension.

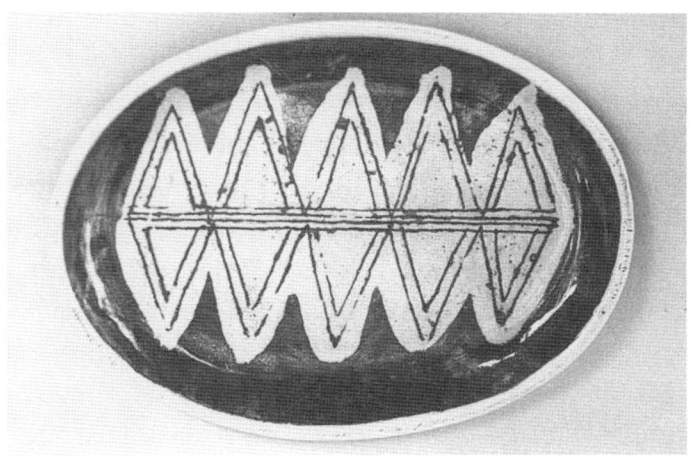

A Moulded Dish

13. THE ALLOTMENT

Chas our neighbour had a large garden in which he grew a lot of flowers and vegetables. In addition he rented an allotment close to the church in which he produced even more vegetables, enough to make him self sufficient. I grew some vegetables in our garden but not nearly enough to feed us through the year. When Chas mentioned that there was an allotment next to his going spare I jumped at the chance to take it on. One of three plots it was larger than a standard allotment and completely grown over. The Church rented it to me for just £9 a year plus an undertaking to help in keeping the footpath to the Church open by cutting back the hedgerows and strimming the grass. There was a shared dilapidated corrugated iron shed in the corner of one of the allotments which could be used to store a few tools and an unusable rain water butt. The stream running alongside the Church path had at one time had been dammed to provide a water supply but for a number of reasons could no longer be used so the only water available was from a tap in the Churchyard several hundred metres away. Despite the lack of irrigation I felt that the plot would enable me to grow enough vegetables to become self-sufficient and perhaps have some over to sell.

The first thing I had to do was to clear the plot of weeds. These seemed to be mainly perennials of the most invasive kind; couch grass, bind weed, thistles, horsetails and ground elder. I didn't want to use any chemical method for getting rid of these nasties but thought a lot of the ground might be cleared by growing potatoes on it. The rest would have to be dug over and the roots removed by hand over a period of time. Having decided what proportion of land I would use for potatoes I then bought tubers of a number of varieties for chitting. Before I could plant them, once they had sprouted, I had to have the land rotorvated. Although this meant that the roots of the weeds would remain in the ground I could plant the potatoes more easily and rely on them to smother the weeds and the rest of the plot was split up into sections for other types of vegetables. To mark out these sections I planted rows of fruit bushes and at the end a number of buddleia trees to attract butterflies. There was one area for peas and beans, another for brassicas and one for root vegetables which could be rotated each year. There was also a permanent bed for the onion family. All these areas were gradually dug over by hand and weeds removed as vegetable seeds were sown or plants set out.

The crops gathered in the first year were terrific. Then things gradually went downhill. In year two there was a drought and despite buckets of water being ferried from the Churchyard tap many plants shrivelled up or didn't set seed. In the year after that potato blight set in which also affected the outdoor tomatoes. Then there were mice eating the broad beans, pigeons stripping the broccoli, wireworm in the main-crop potatoes and sheep getting into the field stripping everything. On top of this the weeds returned with a vengeance. Eventually I came to the conclusion that the allotment required too much time and effort for little return and I gave notice to the Church that I would no longer be renting it. Only a small section of one allotment is worked now. The rest are all overgrown and the tool shed has disappeared into the ground. It has been muted that the allotments will be used as an extension to the church burial ground. What a wonderful place to lay one's bones!

14. MAN'S BEST FRIENDS

When I was younger I much preferred cats to dogs. For all our married life we had at least two cats living with us sometimes three or more. Later on we got friendly with a lady who bred Whippets and I was bowled over by these affectionate graceful animals so it wasn't long before we got our first one. He was a dark coloured whippet called Bruno, a name he came with we decided to keep. He accompanied us on all our holidays in Dorset. He liked travelling about in the car so there was no problem in bringing him when we moved. He quickly settled in to a new life at Trumps In accompanying me on long walks and exploring the local countryside. We were inseparable. Many of the locals loved him and if they saw me without him they would say 'where is Bruno?' He was quite old at the time of the move and had been on medication for a heart condition for a number of years. One day about a year after we came to Whitchurch he suddenly lost the use of his back legs. The Vet gave him an injection which put him on his feet again but warned that he might not have long to live. After that he spent a lot of the time in his basket chewing bones. Whilst this was happening a friend up the road introduced us to a litter of Golden Retriever puppies that had recently been born. Doreen said that she would like to provide a home for one of them but I wasn't keen as the puppies reminded me of a television advert for a well-known brand of toilet paper. I thought that they would leave a lot of hair about the place and anyway I only liked whippets! In the end Doreen's wishes prevailed and we took home a female puppy we decided to call Tess after the heroine in Thomas Hardy's novel. Bruno and Tess hit it off together, the elderly dog and puppy sitting side by side in their baskets chewing bones. Sadly shortly after this Bruno died and was buried in the garden.

Tess now took over from Bruno on my daily walks. She seemed tireless even on the longest of treks and unlike whippets she would not chase everything she saw along the way. Splashing through water, getting muddy and swimming in ponds or the sea was amongst her favourite pursuits and being with people was another. We could take her anywhere. At village events and craft fairs she would lie down patiently by our side all day if necessary. If we said to her 'would you like to go to the pub?' she would rush to the entrance of the Five Bells when we opened the front door. She loved travelling in the car. She was a wonderful companion popular with everyone. The hair she shed however was not so popular. It stopped us from going into some of our friend's houses with her and our vacuum cleaner sucked up a bagful of hair from our carpets nearly every week! This was the only drawback to having her and when measured against the pluses seemed insignificant. She was with us for ten marvellous years. When she died we decided that we would not have another Goldie. We considered her a one off who we will never forget. There are lots of memories. One of my favourites is of her sitting patiently in a sheet designed to protect her after an operation which we called her pyjamas.

A couple of years after Tess came to us a local lady, who we got to know quite well later, called to say that she was the local Whippet Rescue representative and that she had a litter of whippet puppies in her van outside. We said that we really didn't want to take on another dog but she persuaded us to take a look at them however and we went out to the van. There she had four well-grown puppies, three dogs and a bitch. Evidently the puppies had been tied up with rope around their necks and left. They were all the same colour which we later learned was known as brindle. One look was enough. We agreed to give a home to one of the males who was probably the runt of the litter. He didn't have a name so we decided to call him Oliver after the foundling hero in Dickens's novel. He soon settled in and before long was coming with Tess on our walks. He was a gentle placid dog who soon became well known in the village. Like her he was very fond of the pub and soon both dogs would find their way there. In later years Oliver developed a cough for which the Vet could not identify a cause. We felt that it may have originated from the time he was tied up as a puppy and would probably last for the rest of his life. Other than that he is pretty fit.

Shortly after Tess died we thought it might be a good idea if we got another companion for Oliver. As we were now members of The Whippet Rescue, we decided to take on another rescued whippet. Doreen had a word with them and they put us in touch with a lady in Cornwall who bred whippets. She had a dog who wasn't good enough to show which she wanted to find a home for. It was arranged that we would pick up the dog at the motorway services near Taunton. There we spotted this perfect fawn coloured whippet being walked about the service area on a lead. We introduced ourselves and were then introduced to John the whippet who was handed over to us. He was very frightened and on the way back to Trumps In he was very sick in the back of the car. However once he got to the cottage he quickly settled in and hit it off with Oliver. We didn't like the name John but were loath to change it completely Doreen hit on the name Jonty which was the first name of a well known radio correspondent of the day. Before coming to us Jonty had been fed on a mainly vegetarian diet and a check up by the Vet revealed that he was not in a very good healthy state. His teeth were particularly bad and the Vet was of the opinion that he would have lost them if he had gone on with a vegetarian diet for much longer After a few weeks with us however his health improved and his teeth saved. It was some time later that we discovered that he had a more worrying problem. On his first visit to the pub with Oliver he started barking at other dogs there, then he had a fight with a local farmer's collie. We realised we had taken on, what was a so unusual thing, an aggressive whippet. The Vet thought that he had been attacked as a puppy and now had to attack first. He was so marvellous with people however and so we decided to keep him. We are still wary about him with other dogs, but he is so wonderful with people and we love him.

Tess in Her Pyjamas

15. PHOTOGRAPHING BUTTERFLIES

A Speckled Wood Butterfly

In an earlier chapter I mentioned that when I first started photographing butterflies it was a very hit and miss affair. I experimented with various techniques to get close enough to these lovely insects without disturbing them. In addition to trying to get a large image I needed it to be crisp as well. One possibility that I tried was to use a compact camera with a macro setting, but often the viewfinder cut off part of the image and there was not sufficient depth of field to give a crisp picture. Then I tried a single lens reflex camera that was fitted with a telephoto lens and a close-up attachment which enabled me to get large images but they were not all that sharp. The trouble seemed to be that in order to get sufficient light for a good exposure the aperture had to be set at maximum with consequent loss of depth of field. To overcome this problem I experimented with several kinds of flashgun and eventually settled on one that gave enough light to enable me to use the smallest aperture on the lens. I have now used this technique successfully for a number of years.

Some species of butterfly have several broods a year, others have only one. This determines to a certain extent the periods that they can be seen to photograph. Two common spring butterflies to be found in the Marshwood Vale are the Orange Tip and the Brimstone. The former only has one brood a year and is on the wing from late April to mid June and its caterpillars feed on such short lived spring flowering plants as Garlic Mustard and Ladies Smock. The Brimstone however is on the wing in April/May and again in August /September. Some of the late summer ones hibernate and lay eggs the following spring and their larvae feed on either Purging Buckthorn or Alder Buckthorn which are in leaf from April to October in Dorset. Sometimes the caterpillars of multi brood species feed on different food plants at different times of the year. The Holly Blue is a good example of this. In spring its caterpillars usually feed on Holly leaves and in the autumn Ivy leaves, so the availability of the preferred food plant will also determine where a particular species of butterfly might be seen.

Over the years I have got to know when and where I might see particular species of butterfly locally with a view to photographing them. Eventually I got round to creating a table which listed all the butterflies that might occur around Whitchurch, together with details of when and where they might be seen. This was published in the Parish Magazine, together with guidelines on photographing these beautiful creatures, where it created a lot of interest. Later the article was printed in a Butterfly Conservation Society Newsletter. One butterfly that didn't appear on the table was the Wood White. This is a rare butterfly and only two colonies were known in Dorset both nowhere near this end of the county. One day I received a telephone call to say that two specimens had been seen in nearby Prime Coppice, This was a disused coppice but local thatchers had recently cleared an area to grow hazel for thatching spars and this had created the right conditions for the Wood White and some Fritillaries to flourish again. Unfortunately this was a false dawn as the cleared coppice was allowed to become overgrown again when the thatchers used another source to supply their spars.

A Silver Washed Fritillary Butterfly
Feeding on Bramble Blossom

16. VILLAGE EVENTS

Every year in the village there are a number of well-established annual events. These include the Church Fete, the Festival of Flowers, the Blessing of the Animals, the Shave Cross Marathon, the Gymkhana, the Christmas Pudding Stir, the Arts and Crafts Exhibition, the Village Flower Show and Bonfire Night. In addition there are several events of a more sporadic nature such as Jumble Sales, Village Entertainments, Dances, Concerts and Amateur Dramatics often arranged to raise funds for the Village Hall. In fact there were so many events that we didn't have time to go to all of them, or get involved, even if we had wanted to.

The event that probably attracts the most people is the annual Flower Show. It is held on Summer Bank Holiday Monday in a marquee at the back of the Village Hall with some exhibits in the hall itself. This date and venue have been used since the early 1970s but the origins of the show itself go back to 1874. Although it is called the flower show the various classes of exhibits cover fruit, vegetables, home produce (jams, bread, cakes etc.), honey, wine, handicrafts, photography and floral arrangements. There are also a number of children's classes. Apart from the exhibits there are side-shows and other fund raising stalls. Doreen and I have both regularly taken part in this event either as exhibitors or helpers. For a number of years I took my portable potter's wheel to the show to give some simple pottery lessons to both children and adults. I have also been on the Flower Show Committee since the early nineties.

SOUVENIR PROGRAMME
WHITCHURCH, MORCOMBELAKE & RYALL
MILLENNIUM FLOWER SHOW

including:
VEGETABLES – FRUIT – PRODUCE
HANDICRAFTS AND PHOTOGRAPHY

Classes 1 to 47 restricted to residents of
Whitchurch, Morcombelake and Ryall.
Classes 48 to 141 – Open Classes.

TO BE HELD ON

BANK HOLIDAY MONDAY
AUGUST 28th, 2000

AT

WHITCHURCH VILLAGE HALL

2.00 p.m. to 5.00 p.m.
Admission £1 Children Free

**TEAS WILL BE PROVIDED – ICES AND SOFT DRINKS
HOME-MADE CAKES, SWEETS,
BOTTLE AND COUNTRY PRODUCE STALLS,
COMPETITIONS,
CHILDREN'S SPORTS AND GAMES (weather permitting)
FAMILY DOG SHOW**

**For Flower Show Information telephone:
Chideock 489082.
Dog Show Information telephone:
Chideock 489725 (Pat Weeks)**

Entries must be handed in to "The Oak Tree", Whitchurch
(next to Village Hall);
P.O., Morcombelake or Five Bells, Whitchurch,
by **8 p.m. Thursday evening, August 24th.**
Under no circumstances will late entries be accepted.

A Flower Show Programme Cover

The Gymkhana, another well-attended event, started life locally as the Char Valley Horse Show in the late nineteen twenties and quickly developed into a much bigger event. Now it is held in late June in a field close to our garden. There are competitions for all kinds of horses and ponies including jumping, trotting, musical chairs and fancy dress. It is a very popular show especially with the children and the organisers like to invite a few charity and craft stalls to the Gymkhana to add to its attraction. Most years both of us have set up stalls to sell bric-brac, pottery, books and plants. The day of the Gymkhana seems always to be sunny, always enjoyable and always well attended. Long may it continue!

The other major event in the village is the Church Fete. This is usually held in the ground of the Rectory with sometimes a spill over into the Church Square. The day and time that it is held have tended to vary over the years and on occasions the weather has marred it. Generally however it is an enjoyable event which raises a good amount of money for church funds. There are usually more sideshows, games and stalls than at any other annual event in the village. Over the years I have been involved with either the plant stall or sold pottery and Doreen has helped out wherever help is needed.

All these events provide a good opportunity for socialising and we have both made friends at them. Village life is very much enhanced by them and they provide a good opportunity to catch up on local news.

17. THATCH AND THATCHERS

Thatched roofs need a lot of attention. Shortly after moving we found out that ours required a new ridge, a job that has to be done about every ten years. We were advised to contact a local man who had a good reputation as a thatcher. When I spoke to him, he told me that as a young boy he had seen thatchers working on the roof of our cottage, and that this had inspired him to take up the craft himself. He also said that his father had been born in our main bedroom so he had a special affection for Trumps In. He now has a number of men working for him, many of whom are related. We have used him a number of times since then although he hasn't always been easy to get hold of. As a master thatcher he is a very sought after man and has been involved in such projects as thatching the new Globe Theatre in London.

The material used for thatching in the past has usually been Norfolk reed or wheat reed. In the old days Norfolk reed had a life of about a hundred years, but now its life is much shorter because of the modern fertilisers used by farmers which run off the land into the marshes where the reeds grow. Some new buildings are now thatched with reed that comes from Turkey where nitrates are not used so freely. In Dorset however, listed buildings have to be thatched with wheat reed which has a life of about twenty-five years. The spars which are used to fix the thatch to the roof are cut from hazel bushes that have been coppiced, i.e. cut back, so that they provide a number of side shoots which are the right size to cut spars from. Our thatcher grows his own wheat straw without artificial fertilizers and his workers cut their own spars. Both will last the full course.

It is amazing how much material is used in thatching a roof. Shortly after we moved there was a very fierce storm which ripped off the back roof of Chas's cottage next door. All the reed blew over into our patio and was more than two feet deep and when taken away filled several large trailers. Similar trailers full of new wheat reed were needed to replace it. The amount of material that has to be supplied to rethatch a roof and the removal and disposal of the old thatch, makes the upkeep of a thatched building quite expensive. It is quite difficult to know just when it is necessary to renew our thatch. On one occasion water started coming into one of our upstairs bedrooms. On another starlings started pulling off some tired thatch to feed off the maggots that had infested it. At this moment only a quarter of our roof is likely to need attention in the near future. The rest has been renewed since we moved in.

Listening to the thatchers talking to one and another when they worked on our roof gave me an insight into the lovely Dorset dialect. At first I rarely understood what was being said but it was very easy on the ear. Later I got to know some of the expressions. Newcomers to the village such as myself were referred to as Grockles and holiday makers were referred to as Emmetts. The phrase 'it fell apart' became 'Ee cum to pieces'. The thing I liked the most about the dialect was the practice of referring to items as he or she rather than it. For instance if the thatchers were talking about a screwdriver that was too small for the job, they would say 'he won't do that'. If the wood in which a nail was being hammered into was likely to split, they might say 'she won't take that'; an interesting link to several European languages that use masculine and feminine genders for their nouns.

18. NEW POTTERY IDEAS

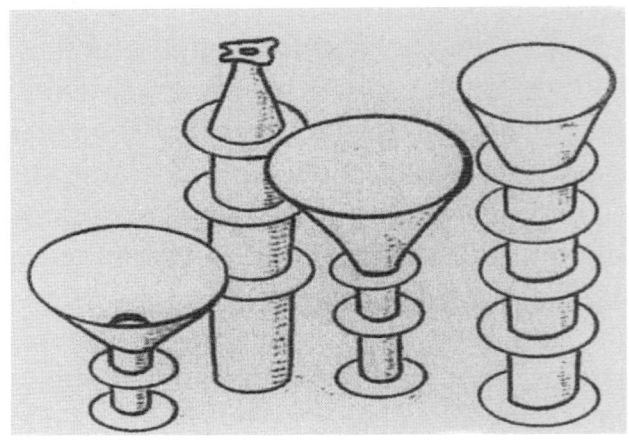

Preliminary Sketches

At the same time as making "bread and butter pots" for sale I was giving thoughts to how I might develop some more individual ceramics to show at exhibitions. On many occasions in the past I had been enthralled with the idea of joining several thrown forms together to form a pot. For the first efforts I threw all the sections on the wheel but later I decided that I should use a combination of thrown and slip-caste sections to achieve the results that I was after. Basically I wanted to create tall forms made up of cast cylinders of various heights with one or two centimetre flanges at the top. These were joined together to form most of the body of each pot and then topped with a thrown section such as a bottle, vase, bowl or jug which gave an identity to it. At first I had difficulties joining thrown and cast sections together even though they were made of the same clay. The joints would split apart in the biscuit firing and could not be mended with biscuit stopping. Luckily I came across a recipe for a jointing paste that was used by commercial potteries to attaché handles to mugs before they were fired, and with a slight modification I made up a recipe that solved my problem. Soon I had built up a collection of these tiered pots and wondered how I could exhibit them.

Two painters who exhibited regularly at the village hall Arts and Crafts exhibitions had seen some of my new style pots and suggested that we might have a joint exhibition of our work. They also said that they knew of a third painter who would like to take part. We discussed various venues but decided that the village hall would be a good choice. It was relatively inexpensive to rent and it had a lot of stands for hanging paintings on as well as tables that could be used to display pots. It also had plenty of space to park cars so we agreed that, provided that the exhibition was well advertised, we should go ahead with it. One of the painters managed to get an article about our work in Dorset Life Magazine together with a photograph of us. I prepared a press release for our local newspaper and also got some posters and private view cards reproduced.

It was quite exciting setting up the exhibition. The painters had a good selection of framed paintings which filled all of the hanging space in the hall. In addition they were all able to put a number of unframed paintings which were put in a trough near the entrance to the exhibition. For my part I was able to provide more than fifty of my new style pots many of which were quite tall. It was suggested that these pots might be displayed on the hall stage rather than on separate tables. This seemed a good idea which I readily accepted as it seemed to link the pottery to the paintings very well. The final layout looked quite stunning.

We invited more than two hundred people to the Private View. Most of them turned up. Sales of paintings were very good but pottery sales were disappointing. Putting a price on the pots had been difficult. I hadn't aimed high but I thought that I should charge more for my new work than I had expected from my bread and butter work. Compared with the prices the paintings were sold for mine were modest. I sold enough work to cover my costs but that was about all. One important thing came out of this first exhibition however. I overheard a teenager saying to her parents that my new pots reminded her of pagodas. This expression struck a chord with me and from that point on I referred to these pots as 'Pagoda Pots'.

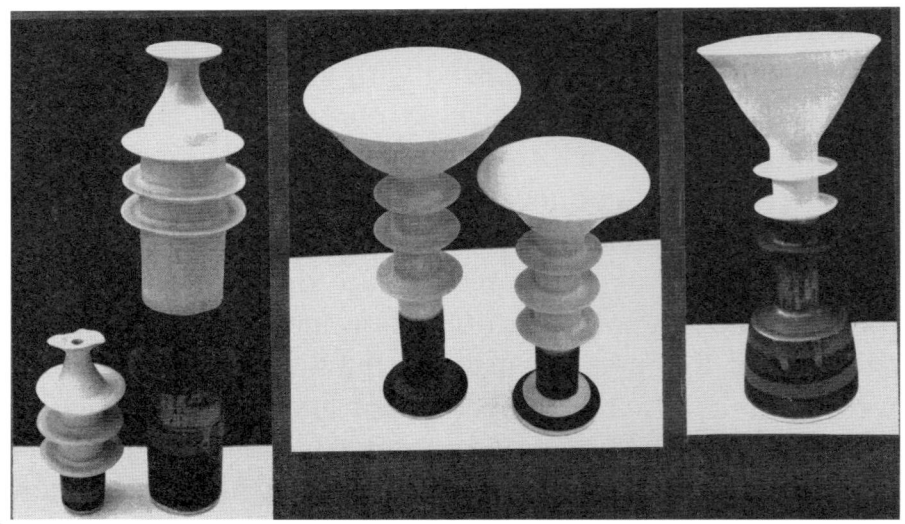

Some Pagoda Pots

19. WILD FLOWERS

Ladies Smock

Before I moved from London to Dorset I had little interest in wild flowers. I had some vague childhood memories about daisy chains and reflecting buttercups to determine whether I liked butter, but apart from that, wild flowers were a complete mystery to me. When I came to Whitchurch, all this changed. The local hedgerow verges were full of all kinds of flowering plants in every season of the year and I was mesmerized by this and wanted to know what each flower was called. One way of identifying them I thought might be to take photographs of the individual flowers in close-up and then look them up in a suitable handbook. This was easier said than done. There are possibly scores of different wild flowers to be seen in the Marshwood Vale throughout the year and it was not possible to photograph all of these so I decided that I would concentrate on the more numerous varieties. This approach has worked well and I am now familiar with most of the common wild flowers to be seen locally. The camera

I used first of all was the one that I took my close-up butterfly pictures on i.e. the old manual single reflex camera with an extension ring and a fairly primitive flashgun. Things have now moved on in terms of automatic functioning and I went along with this firstly to a new up to date single lens reflex camera and recently a digital one. The digital camera has many advantages over the others in that it can focus down to one centimetre from a flower and it is possible to see the results immediately and to correct every image on the computer before printing it.

Going through the year the first hedgerow wild flowers usually to be seen are snowdrops. In February these are followed by the yellow flowered primroses, coltsfoot and lesser celandine. In March and April there is a profusion of the white blossoms of greater stitchwort, wild garlic and garlic mustard. In parts of Dorset April is the month to see large areas covered with cowslips but locally I have only seen them in small numbers. June brings forth the tricolour of white oxeye daisies and cow parsley, the blue of bluebells and the dark pink of red campion and foxgloves. Later in the year the blues of knapweed, tufted vetch and various thistles predominate inter-dispersed with the white fluffy beards of meadowsweet. Come late summer the yellows return in the form of fleabane and ragwort. Hedgerow verges are usually trimmed in early July and it may be mid August before they have a new flush of wild flowers. Some verges are set aside and not cut however because of their special wild flower interest. They are usually marked in Dorset by blue painted posts at the beginning and end of each protected verge. On these sites there are lots of different species to be seen all throughout the summer. Before the introduction of specific herbicides most meadows would also have had a marvellous display of wild flowers before they were cut for hay. These included poppies, corn cockles, snakehead fritillaries, ragged robin, meadow buttercup, bugle and various thistles. The list is endless. There are still a few meadows in the Vale that have a good display of these plants but the majority just have a single type of grass growing. Things might be changing however as more land is being set aside to support wildlife. Certainly the areas where wild flowers are given a free reign are growing in the Vale. It is very difficult to commit to paper the joy these wild flowers arouse. They have obviously been a source of inspiration to many poets, writers and artists. In Dorset Thomas Hardy has described them in his novels and William Barnes in his local dialect poems. For me they have added an extra dimension to my appreciation of the natural world.

Knapweed

20. BRIDPORT ARTS CENTRE

Bridport Arts Centre is a thriving organisation situated in an attractive converted chapel in South Street. It has a large theatre where many events are held, e.g. live music, drama, dance, film and children's workshops. It also has a café and bar plus three galleries which are used for all kinds of exhibitions. The largest gallery is on the first floor and is named after the late Kenneth Allsop a well-known correspondent who played an important role in setting up the Arts Centre. It is well lit and airy. There is space for a large number of paintings to be hung on its walls and a correspondently large floor area which can accommodate three dimensional exhibits on plinths. One of the smaller galleries is situated at the rear of the building which doubles as a café area and overlooks an attractive walled garden. The third gallery is situated in the foyer. These smaller galleries are mainly used for displaying two-dimensional exhibits. Each year the Arts Centre runs an important International Creative Writing Competition and also an Open Art Competition which is open to all professional and amateur artists living in the south west. They also run craft and farmers' markets during the busy holiday periods.

I have been a member of the Centre since I came to Dorset and have been involved with it in a number of ways over the years. Shortly after the move we provided a notice board outside Trumps In on which we displayed posters about the events that were being held there. We regularly booked a table at the craft fairs and attended theatre events and private views. Later I rented the Allsop Gallery for an exhibition of work by myself and the three painters I had exhibited with at the Whitchurch Village Hall. This was very successful and we had many more visitors and sales than we had at the earlier exhibition. The ambiance of the Gallery was really stunning and made me determined to arrange further exhibitions there. What I didn't know at the time was that I would become much more involved with the Centre. Also I didn't know then that I would form the Dorset Pottery Group and that we would hold many meetings and exhibitions there. I certainly didn't know that the pottery group would create a large ceramic sculpture of an ammonite to celebrate the second millennium, or that it would be erected in the garden at the rear of the Arts Centre and become a tourist attraction. But these things did happen!

21. DORSET POTTERY GROUP

In the early Nineties one of my closest friends who was living in Sussex, invited me to a 'potters day' that had been arranged by the Wealdon Potters. This was a pottery group to which he belonged who had invited a well known potter to give a demonstration of his work. On the same day they had also arranged for a local Japanese lady to demonstrate what was involved in the Japanese Tea Ceremony. I was highly fascinated by this and thought about the possibility of forming a pottery group in Dorset and arranging similar demonstrations. I also thought that it might be possible to buy materials in bulk, or at a discount, and share the savings. Collective marketing might also be arranged and exhibition space shared.

I decided to put up posters locally and spread the word around my friends but I didn't have much response. Finally five of us got together at the George Inn in Bridport and decided to go ahead with forming a group anyway. We notified the local press and 'Ceramic Review' that the Dorset Pottery Group had been formed and within a few weeks we had more than twenty members. Membership eventually rose to seventy. This membership had a wide spread of skills ranging from self-taught potters, who enjoyed the craft as a hobby, to others who were fully professional and make a living from their pots. At an early meeting of members it was decided that they did not want a formal elected committee for the Group but would prefer it to be run informally. It was also agreed that there would not be an annual membership fee and that we would be funded by members donating postage stamps and monies collected at Group events. Compared with other UK pottery groups this was a unique method of funding and meant that members would only pay towards the cost of the events attended. From the beginning I agreed to become the Honorary Secretary of the Group which entailed arranging a programme of events, drafting and distributing two Newsletters each year, together with handling financial matters and publicity. At that time I didn't realise what a lot of work this would involve. It was a steep learning curve!

The first thing that had to be arranged was a venue that would be suitable for an exhibition of members' work. The obvious place was the Allsop Gallery in Bridport Arts Centre which was large enough to accommodate a lot of work of each of the twenty-five members who had expressed a wish to exhibit. I was also familiar with the booking arrangements having exhibited there previously myself. So I made a tentative booking for two weeks at the end of October. This was a good time because it covered the autumn half term when a lot of visitors came to Bridport. Once a booking had been made, the next thing was to decide how much space could be allocated to each exhibitor, and what stands would need to be provided as the Art Centre only had a limited number of plinths to offer. After some deliberations with a few members we decided that each exhibitor could have a floor area roughly eight by four feet and that they would each provide three sheets of white or black painted chipboard to cover this area. They were also asked to supply stands for these boards and any additional plinths that they were able to provide. It was also agreed that there would be no selection procedure and that there would be a minimum price for exhibits. The latter was agreed because it would enable many of the amateur members to exhibit but, at the same time, avoid the show looking just like another craft market.

Details of these arrangements were published in the summer newsletter and press releases were sent to the local press, radio, TV and pottery journals. After that it was just a matter of waiting to see how things would turn out.

What in fact turned out far exceeded expectations! The local press were ecstatic about it and the following is an extract from their report: -

'Artfully placed lighting reflects the myriad colours of ceramics of the Dorset Pottery Group's first exhibition being staged in the Allsop Gallery at Bridport Arts Centre. Professional and amateur work is displayed side by side, set out on white boards and plinths at varying levels for maximum viewing effect, while overhead hang mobiles, composed of many small pots strung from the rafters. As a first exhibition it is very expressive and deserves plenty of support for the craftsmen and craftswomen of the Dorset Pottery Group.'

The annual exhibition is now a regular event in Dorset. On a couple of occasions it has been shown on television. During the summer months I arranged a number of pottery events for the Group. These included raku firings, where members and visitors could glaze biscuit pots and have them fired, pottery making days, plaster casting on various local beaches and kiln firing weekends. The latter were held in the grounds of the Five Bells Inn. Over the years we experimented with a number of different kilns at these events which are detailed in a later chapter. As the Group became better known, I got involved with a lot of correspondence from abroad about pottery matters and also swapped Newsletters with most of the other pottery associations in the UK. This was a lot of work for one person and kept me very busy. However they were heady days and it didn't seem too much to handle until I got deeply involved in a project to celebrate the Millennium. More about that in a separate chapter.

Dorset Pottery Group
Newsletter

NEWSLETTER No 8

DECEMBER 1996

PREPARING FOR THE MILLENIUM

A recent article in 'Studio Pottery ' suggested that the year 1999-2000 will provide potters with an unprecedented opportunity for making commemorative souvenirs. It queried whether potters had even begun to address the potential demand. There are now less than 900 working days to go! This will be discussed at our first 1997 meeting. It is hoped to consider not only what individual members might do, but also what the Group as an entity could do to commemorate this historic occasion.

CONTACTS WITH OTHER POTTERY GROUPS IN THE UK

Contacts with other Groups have increased over the past year and we now exchange Newsletters with a number of them. It is hoped to widen these contacts in the future. In a number of cases it has been agreed that other Groups can copy articles from our Newsletters, provided that they are not protected with a copyright symbol and the source is acknowledged.

INTERNATIONAL CONTACTS

These too have increased and we now send copies of our Newsletters to contacts in Spain and Germany. Most of the correspondence is in English but it would be helpful if any member could translate documents if the need arises. Please let me know if you could help in this way.

THE INTERNET

This is increasingly being used by potters, and others with an interest in ceramics, as a means of contact. At the moment the Group has no access to this method of communication but it would be very useful if any member does have access to the Internet and would be prepared to receive or send the occasional e-mail on our behalf. If any member is prepared to do this could they let me have their e-mail address please so that it can be circulated in our next Newsletter.

POSSIBLE STAGING OF A NATIONAL OR INTERNATIONAL EXHIBITION

As most members will know the splendid Allsop Gallery in Bridport Arts Centre provides a wonderful setting for the Groups' Autumn exhibitions. Now that links with other potters have been formed both here and abroad, the question has arisen as to whether it would be possible to arrange a national or international ceramics exhibition there. The Arts Centre are very keen on the idea and it has been circulated recently by means of a Press Release. There seem to be two main questions to be answered before the idea can be got off the ground. Firstly, would enough potters be willing to take part? Secondly, could we get sufficient financial help? This will also be discussed at our first 1997 meeting

Alan Ashpool

①

Front Page of a Dorset Pottery Group Newsletter

22. A GLUT OF FIGS AND WILD MUSHROOMS

In the garden at the rear of Trumps In there is a very large ancient gnarled fig tree. It bears fruit about the size of a conference pear and is coloured yellow when ripe with a lush purple interior. There are many smaller examples of this tree in the village which obviously grew from suckers at the base of our monster. In warmer climes fig trees may produce up to three crops a year but in this country they only produce one. Every autumn, when the leaves fall, the branches of our tree are festooned with hundreds of baby figs. In most years the ravages of winter weather drastically reduce this number and only a few are left in spring to grow on to sizeable fruit. A lot of these are hidden by the large leaves that cover the tree in summer and it is not possible to keep track of many of the fruit as they ripen. In most years the blackbirds and wasps beat us to nearly all of the mature figs. This is annoying because the ripe fruits are absolutely delicious and we would have liked to have given some to our many friends.

One year however, after a very warm winter and a sunny summer, hundreds of figs ripened and we managed to distribute carrier bags full around the Village. Apart from being eaten as a fresh fruit these figs go well with melon, dry cured ham and blue cheese particularly Dorset Blue Vinney. There is a limit to the number that could be eaten in this way however because of their loosening effect on the bowels. A number of methods were devised to deal with the glut. Some were frozen in their raw state. Some were cooked in honey syrup and then frozen. People even tried drying them in the same way as apple rings. In the end it all really got out of hand and many fruits were left to rot. I suppose that with global warming this glut may repeat itself. If it does, I think I will pass the fruit on to a greengrocer and let him deal with it.

When I lived in London I developed an interest in finding and cooking wild mushrooms. This interest was sparked off by a Penguin paperback entitled 'Plats du Jour'. It contained a wonderful chapter about edible fungi and how to cook them. At that time there were very few other books about the subject so it became my bible. Many of the varieties mentioned could be found in the woods and meadows on the outskirts of South East London and it wasn't long before I had tried out some of the recipes contained in the book. The results were fantastic so I invited some of my peers to come and try them. Some liked them. Others were suspicious that they might be poisoned. This was the general feeling some people had at the time about wild mushrooms. Now things are much different and many of the varieties can be bought in supermarkets and delicatessens. There are also many more books about how to identify them and ways of cooking them.

My interest continued when I moved to Dorset. Not many varieties of wild mushrooms turned up however in the lanes and countryside around Whitchurch. There were a few shaggy ink-caps, blewits, giant puffballs, parasols and eared mushrooms but no cepes, chanterelles or morels. There were also very few field mushrooms. I asked a number of locals whether they knew of the whereabouts of any fungi in the area but didn't have much success. Then one year a local farmer ploughed a large field that hadn't been cultivated since the war. A few weeks later the whole field was closely carpeted with field mushrooms. Boxes of mushrooms about two or three cubic feet in volume were bartered for a pint of beer at the Five Bells and carrier bags full of them were left in villagers' porches. They still kept coming up and, as with the glut of figs, other ways of using them had to be devised. Some were dried and many were frozen. Others were incorporated in cooked dishes which could be frozen. Eventually they did stop appearing and have not returned.

23. CLOUDED YELLOWS AND PAINTED LADIES

A few of our butterflies come from warmer climes and are unlikely to survive the mildest of winters. Of these the Red Admirals consistently arrive in fairly large numbers each year. On the other hand the numbers of Clouded Yellows and Painted Ladies fluctuate greatly. My first sightings of Clouded Yellows took place in Kent shortly after the end of the war when I was a child. There was a large influx of this lovely butterfly then and I remember searching for their eggs and caterpillars on lucerne which was a widespread crop at the time. My acquaintance with the Painted Lady took place about the same time when there were hoards of them feeding on purple buddleia flowers which were abundant on old bomb sites in those days. I don't remember seeing many of these butterflies again until I came to Dorset.

Higher counts of Clouded Yellows are said to be made in Dorset than in any other British county. Yet even here the numbers are always erratic. Most years however I have been able to photograph a few specimens. The numbers to be seen increased dramatically in 1996. In that year many immigrants arrived in the spring and laid their eggs on the clovers that are common in Dorset and by late summer their offspring had emerged. There were vast numbers to be seen everywhere in the county. Instead of chasing a rare single specimen to photograph I was able to capture images of several on a single wild flower plant. There had evidently been an even greater number of these butterflies to be seen in 1983. These two 'Clouded Yellow years' are the only ones to have occurred since the huge immigration of 1947 when I had seen them for the first time.

The numbers of Painted Ladies to be seen in Dorset also fluctuates from year to year but not to the same extent as Clouded Yellows. Some are evident in most summers and lately a few have been seen on the wing in spring. Normally this butterfly would not survive the colder months, either as an adult or as a pupa, but with the recent spell of warm winters some have done so. In a few years vast numbers have appeared and it has been possible to photograph groups of these wonderful creatures feeding on the buddleia flowers in our garden. The largest groups arrived in 1996 on southerly winds coming up from North Africa where they normally breed. In that year I spent an early June holiday in Majorca where I spotted almost locust type swarms of them on their way North. From the large numbers seen there it wasn't too difficult to forecast that it would be an exceptional Painted Lady year in England. In fact 1996 was probably the most memorable year of all time for seeing these butterflies.

24. BUYING A PIANO

When I reached 60 and began to draw my Civil Service pension we decided that we could afford some of the things that we were unable to buy earlier. For me I wanted to update my hi-fi and camera. Doreen decided that she would like to have a piano. She had learnt to play in her youth and wanted to take it up again now that she had more time to spare. Living where we did the problem was where could we go to buy one. Unlike London, shops that stocked second-hand pianos were few and far between or didn't exist. Several local newspapers however advertised pianos for sale. Doreen spoke to some of these advertisers, and eventually made an arrangement with a firm in Southampton who said that they would bring a selection of pianos to the cottage so that she could try them out. We were both a bit sceptical about how they would manage this.

A few days later however a large removal van turned up in the evening after dark outside Trumps In and an incredibly dressed man knocked at the door. He wore an ankle length black overcoat over a full evening dress. With him were two other men who looked like archetype furniture removal men. Long black overcoat was obviously in charge and he invited us into the removal van which housed six pianos, of different vintages and prices, which Doreen was invited to try out. Some sounded better than others but eventually she found one she liked. The interior of the van was not very well lit, so it was not possible to look closely at the general condition of the woodwork of the piano she was interested in, so we asked if they could bring it into the cottage. This proved quite difficult because there was a gravel forecourt and I wondered whether, if we didn't buy it, the removal men might not be able to get it back into the van. When it was finally hauled into our lounge, it fortunately did not look too bad. It was scruffy, and needed a little tender loving care, but it sounded good. So we bought it!

Several weeks after we did the deal long black overcoat phoned Doreen and said that for a small fee he would arrange for the piano to be collected and have the woodwork completely renovated. By this time Doreen had given it a good clean and polish herself so we declined the offer. In fact we wondered whether this offer was some kind of scam and the reason that long black overcoat originally turned up in the dark. Generally however, we were very happy with the piano. When we had it tuned, the tuner said it was a good buy. Evidently it was of German origin made by a Herr Steinbach of Berlin around the beginning of the nineteen hundreds, and was worth more than we had paid for it. Since then we have had some remedial work carried out but generally Doreen is very happy with the piano and it has proved to be a success.

25. KILN FIRING EVENTS

Over the years there have been a number of kiln firing events in the grounds at the back of the Five Bells Inn. I originally arranged them for members of the Dorset Pottery Group but later, as they were advertised on local radio and in the press, many local people and holiday makers turned up. The major aims of these events, which normally took place in September and lasted two or three days, was for Group members to finish the pots they had made at our Upwey summer workshops. This was done either by smoke firing or raku glazing them. Each year we tried to improve the results obtained previously and to experiment with further firing methods.

In all four different methods were employed in the first year. These were (a) newspaper kilns; (b) a paper and sawdust kiln in a garden incinerator; (c) a large sawdust kiln, and (d) a ceramic fibre raku kiln designed and made by Fil Cooke. The pots to be fired were generally made of crank body and biscuited to circa 1000 degrees Centigrade. Two or three however were made out of local clay which had only been dried in a domestic oven to about 200 degrees Centigrade. A number of newspaper kilns were fired; all of them based on a design by David Metcalfe which had been published in 'Ceramic Review' but with extra coils added to the tops and bottoms. The pots themselves were wrapped individually in flattened coils. They all burned for over half an hour and a sample pyrometer reading showed a temperature of circa 750 degrees Centigrade in the centre. This was high enough to fix any smoke patterns on the pots which could then be waxed to show them to their best advantage. A raw pot was put into one of these kilns and fired perfectly; but another burst however, possibly because it had not dried out enough.

A Newspaper Kiln Being Fired

The first results from the garden incinerator were disappointing when sawdust was used on its own. It quickly burned through leaving fugitive smoke patterns which rubbed off. But when the pots were wrapped in coils of newspaper and the incinerator lined with paper the results were even more exciting than those obtained in the newspaper kilns. The firings lasted as long, reached similar temperatures and gave identical if not better results. A raw pot was put into one of these firings and came through with flying colours.

The pots fired in Fil Cooke's raku kiln all came out with the splendid results that one had come to expect from his firings. Visitors as well as members could choose a biscuited bowl and paint it with a selection of glazes. They could then watch it being fired, taken out of the kiln whilst it was hot and buried in sawdust so that it would be starved of oxygen so that the clay turned black. Finally it was put into a bowl of water and scrubbed to reveal the magical colours of the glaze. At the second event Fil was able to demonstrate the building of his kiln from scratch which was an added bonus, Later he had the details published in 'Ceramic Review'.

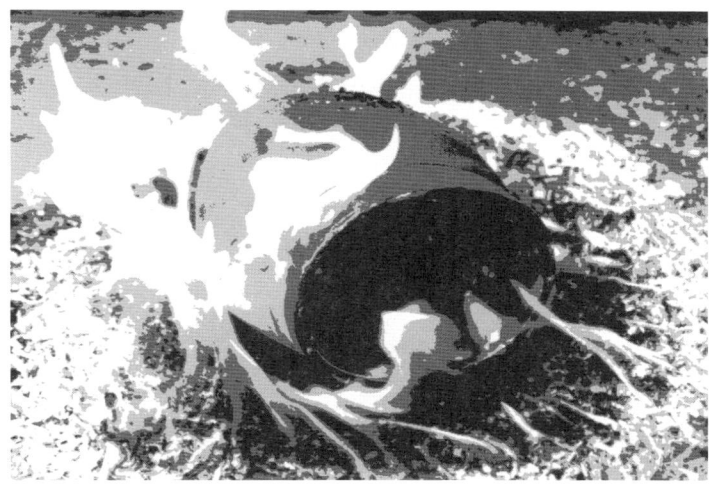

A Raku Pot Reducing in Sawdust

These kiln firing events were held at the Five Bells for six years. During this time there were three different landlords but all of them were happy to hold these events there. Every year I tried to introduce a new kind of firing in addition to the newspaper, sawdust and raku kilns. One year there was an up draught kiln, then there was a copy of a Roman kiln and these were followed in a subsequent year by a pit firing. A local builder offered to help out with the latter by bringing his mechanical digger along to do some of the heavy work. These events came to an end when the

Group decided that we should spend as much time as possible on a millennium project. Many members look back at these events with fond memories, especially of the large friendly goat called 'Trouble' who lived in the pub's garden and who ate our newspapers as soon as we had rolled them up.

Packing the Pit Kiln

26. CIDER MAKERS

My first experience of country cider was in my early twenties when I often went into a local pub after my pottery evening classes. This pub had a separate cider bar full of large barrels of different kinds of cider. There was cloudy, clear, sweet, dry, dark coloured and light coloured cider. At that time there was no duty on it so it cost less than half the price of beer. It was also very strong and as a novice drinker I was often very ill after a session in the cider bar. Because of this I gave it up after a few evenings and didn't touch draught cider again until I moved to Trumps In Cottage.

Dorset is a cider making county and most of it is made by individuals or small groups of village people. Signs offering cider for sale can commonly be seen outside farms and cottages. My introduction to it came about accidentally. One afternoon I went exploring the butterfly life in a local coppice. There I came upon a large green corrugated iron shed in which several men were sitting on a couple of wooden benches passing a large three handled pot around and drinking from it. One of them was the man I had met earlier when Doreen broke her wrist. His name was Alan Pitfield. He invited me over and I was offered a swig from the three handled pot which contained a very strong but pleasant dry cider. We got into conversation and I learnt that the cider was made on site using the local cider apples that grew next to the coppice. Some of it was sweetened with local honey that was added to the apple juice before it was fermented. The apples were collected off of the ground underneath the apple trees in the autumn and chopped up. The juice was then pressed out of the apple pulp by means of a cider press. Alternate layers of pulp and straw were built up on the bottom bed of the press and, when they reached a certain height, the top bed of the press was screwed down manually so that it squeezed all of the juice out of the pulp. The press used at the coppice was quite large and had two screws so a lot of juice could be extracted in one pressing. The pressed juice was put into large oak barrels and honey was added to some of the barrels to give a sweeter taste. The juice was then left to ferment. No yeast was added to the barrels as the natural yeasts that existed in the apple skins were sufficient to start the fermentation process going. Once this had finished, the young cider was transferred to other barrels and left to mature.

For several years after I discovered the green hut I spent quite a few happy hours there sharing in the cider and conversation. Alan was very knowledgeable about the natural history of the coppice and talked about the swarms of butterflies that could be seen there before active coppicing ceased. Sadly he has passed on. The green hut is now in ruins and the cider press and barrels are no longer there. I still visit the coppice from time to time for a walk down memory lane.

27. NATURE NOTES

Our Parish Magazine is published every month and covers the whole of the Marshwood Vale. It mainly deals with church matters but villagers can get articles or information published in it about any subject. As mentioned earlier my list of local butterflies was published in it and some time after this the Editor of the magazine actively sought articles for inclusion because insufficient copy was coming forward. At that time there was quite a lot being written about the effects of global warming so I decided to write an article for the magazine about its possible effects on local flora and fauna. The article pointed out how certain wild flowers, insects and amphibians were appearing earlier and earlier each year and suggested that this might be due to global warming. I did not see myself as a naturalist but rather as a nature lover, so I made the article as simple as possible leaving out any technical or scientific facts. It was illustrated with a simple line drawing of red admiral butterflies sipping nectar from wildflowers. For want of a better title I called it 'Nature Notes'. The article was accepted and duly published in the magazine. It was warmly received and several people phoned me and asked whether I could write any more articles. So 'Nature Notes' was born.

For the first couple of years I wrote an article every two months. The subject varied greatly but there was a standard layout on an A5 page with several illustrations down the left-hand side. Again they were warmly received by magazine readers and I came under pressure to write an article on a regular monthly basis. Finding completely different subjects to write about each month, and also illustrations about those subjects, entailed a lot of research on my part but I also learnt a lot about nature that had passed me by earlier. These discoveries included fiction, poems, music and folklore about nature. There were sayings about the weather, the time of year and church festivals, as well as more down to earth matters such as what food to eat, what trees to plant, or how birds and butterflies might be attracted to the garden. I also found out a lot about the need for action to preserve the many species that are under threat because of the way we farm, hunt, fish or cut down trees for timber. This need for action also encompassed global warming, a subject I often returned to, which was seen as the greatest threat to many species. There were a few local success stories however. In Dorset these included a campaign to save the water vole from disappearing completely and another to keep track of a decreasing number of brown hares.

I continue to get people contacting me about various aspects of subjects raised in Nature Notes. In some cases I can help right away, but if not I try to find an answer by further research. The learning process continues! Recently I became involved in The Living Churchyards Project. This is a project set up by the Dorset Wildlife Trust to encourage wildlife in many of Dorset's old churchyards. Our wonderful churchyard of St. Candida and Holy Cross has been accepted as the Best Newcomer to the Project.

28. GARDEN PONDS

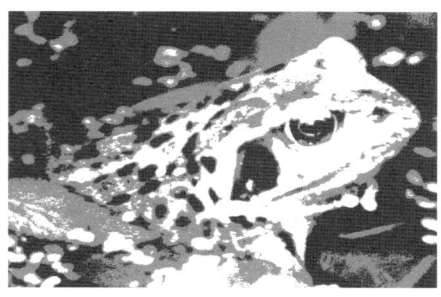

In several Nature Notes I wrote about ponds and the creatures that lived in them as this has been another lifetime passion with me. In my London garden I excavated a pond shortly after moving. It was situated just a few yards from our dinning room window so we had a birds eye view of a lot of the wildlife it attracted. It was lined with butyl rubber which has quite a long life and was still functioning, according to the purchasers of our London house, for quite a few years after we left. For vegetation I planted some native yellow flags as marginals, some Canadian pond weed as an oxygenator and water hyacinth to provide some floating leaves. These soon established themselves and spread fairly rapidly. As if by magic in the early spring of the following year clumps of frogs' spawn appeared in the water. I also obtained a small amount of toads' spawn locally and put that in the pond. Hundreds of tadpoles hatched out and many turned into young adults. A number of newts turned up in the summer and started laying their single eggs in the leaves of the Canadian pondweed. These I identified as smooth newts and palmate newts. Both species became regular inhabitants living in the water in spring and summer then, after breeding, leaving the pond to feed off of the land until they hibernated for the winter. Lots of water insects and molluscs soon turned up, again as if by magic, and colonised the pond. In reality they were probably imported in the water plants. There were pond skaters who lived on the water surface, water beetles who lived below the surface and water shrimps who lived in the mud at the bottom of the pond, giant water snails and the smaller ramshorn type appeared together with a number of bivalves. Some of the most interesting insects were dragonflies and damselflies. I found it more fascinating seeing them hatch from the larvae than it was watching a butterfly emerging from a chrysalis. The larvae, which looked like a scorpion, would climb up the leaf of a yellow flag and appear to die. Some time later however its back would split open and a bejewelled adult dragonfly would emerge. Magic stuff!

My London pond was one of the few things I missed when I moved to Dorset. So, shortly after the move, it became a priority to install a new pond in the garden at the rear of Trumps In. Because of the clayey soil in the area I wondered whether I could puddle a pond without the need of a liner. This was not possible however as the soil at the rear of the cottage was predominately porous green sand so, I went back to good old butyl, The finished pond measured eight feet by five feet and was eighteen inches deep in the middle. To allow for the planting of marginals and other water plants it was terraced upwards to the sides. Once filled with water the liner fitted snugly to the various contours. I purchased some water plants from a local garden centre and got permission from a local farmer to transplant some others from a stream in one of his fields. It was late summer so they quickly established themselves and before long, as with the London pond, all kinds of wildlife started to appear. There were pond-skaters, water-boatmen, water beetles, freshwater shrimps, various kinds of molluscs and leeches. When the next spring arrived a number of frogs turned up and laid numerous clumps of spawn. No toads appeared however. They seem to prefer larger and deeper ponds to spawn in, especially if it was the pond they grew up in. As an experiment I transplanted some toad spawn in the pond, and although the tadpoles hatched from it grew into toads none ever returned to spawn themselves. The only other amphibians to turn up were a few palmate newts. They readily breed in the pond and over the years their numbers have increased. Dragonflies and Damsel flies also breed successfully.

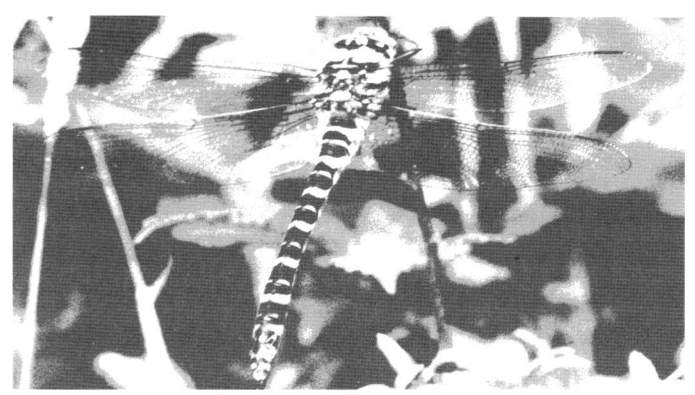

A Newly Hatched Dragonfly

29. THE TWO MARMALADES AND OTHER CATS

As I mentioned earlier for all of our married life we have had at least two cats and sometimes three or four. When we moved to Dorset we brought an elderly tabby called Sophie and a young black cat called Polly. Sophie had been with us for fourteen years or so but Polly was still almost a kitten who had turned up at our London house one day and stayed. A year or so after we moved, one of Doreen's friends from her library days sent us a video of two kittens that they were trying to find a home for. Doreen was besotted with them and so we had four cats again, one was a tortoiseshell female who we called Cosette and the other a black and white tom who we named Troy. Sophie wasn't with us very long before she succumbed to old age and sadly she was followed after a year or so by Cosette who developed an inoperable tumour. The other two were with us for very much longer but eventually they too passed away.

Doreen couldn't bear to be in a cottage without cats so she started looking around for another one and I suggested that this time it would be nice to have a ginger tom for a change. A neighbour said that there was an advert in a local paper by the Cat Protection League looking for a suitable home for a two year old ginger tom and his sable coloured sister. Evidently these siblings had been re-advertised for several months so we wondered whether there was some problem with them. It transpired that their keepers were concerned that the couple should be adopted by a family that wasn't living near a busy road, as the cats were not familiar with traffic. It seemed to them that our cottage might be suitable because of its rural situation and we made arrangements for our cottage and garden to be given a look over. The lady who came was impressed with both, so arrangements were made for us to meet the cats.

What we hadn't expected was the reception we got from the siblings when we met up with them. They were housed together in a spacious cattery type enclosure in the garden. The sable coloured female, called Missy, was very beautiful and was quite approachable but her ginger brother, called Ginge, was quite ugly and hissed when approached. We thought that he may be the reason why the pair had not been relocated earlier. Their keepers wanted them to be kept together and whilst many people would be willing to take on Missy they would probably have been put off by Ginge. Our experience with rescue dogs however, had taught us that although there would be problems when taking them on, the love and pleasure that they gave far outweighed the difficulties. So we both felt that taking on these cats would not be dissimilar and as far a we were concerned there was only the paper work to be done. There were documents that confirmed that both cats had been micro chipped, neutered and inoculated. We signed papers to say how we would look after them and invited to make a small donation to the Cats Protection League if we wanted to. They really do look after their cats! Missy and Ginge were put into a basket and we set off for home.

What a journey it turned out to be! I sat with the cat basket in the back seat. Missy was very frightened and it wasn't very long before she was sick all over the place, then when she had enough of that she started to defecate. Ginge spent all of his time trying to get out of the basket and trod all over the deposits his sister had made. The smell was unbelievable. When we got them home we put them in the spare bedroom where we had left litter trays and toys. There we offered them some food and water but they were not interested and disappeared under the bed. They kept this up for a couple of days but eventually curiosity got the better of them and they started looking out of the window overlooking the garden. They first thing they saw were the two whippets which caused them to hide under the bed again for another two days. Then we coaxed them down to the garden and tried to introduce them to the dogs who were kept on their leads. The dogs barked and tried to chase them so the cats rushed upstairs and hid under the bed yet again. At that point we decided that we were unlikely to be able to bring the cats and dogs together in the same way as with previous animals, so we devised a new regime that meant that the dogs would no longer be able to go into the back garden. They would be taken for extra walks each day and allowed to spend more time with us in the house. They seemed to like the changes. Gradually the cats bonded to us and it was a joy to see both playing in garden. It must have been magic for them after spending so long penned up. There were some setbacks when the dogs inadvertently got into the garden and chased them but by and large the new arrangements worked well.

The cats are now well settled and I have nicknamed them 'the two marmalades'. Individually we have renamed them as we didn't like their original names. Ginge is now called 'Caspar' and Missy 'Clio'. We both love them to pieces.

30. THE BRIDPORT AMMONITE

A couple of years before the Millennium the 'Studio Pottery Magazine' suggested that potters should be thinking about what they might make to celebrate it. I put this to Dorset Pottery Group members in a newsletter and suggested that any ideas that they might have could be considered at the next meeting. About twenty members came along and many ideas were put forward ranging from commemorative mugs to large pieces of sculpture. There was no consensus however until somebody suggested that we should make a large ammonite and another member suggested that this should be a three dimensional piece. Yet another suggested that the larger segments of the ammonite should be decorated with scenes depicting the history of Dorset on a theme 'back through the ages'. Most of the members present endorsed these ideas and I agreed to do some preliminary planning for the project.

From the very beginning I felt that the sculpture would have to be made in sections so that it could easily be transported and would fit into an electric kiln of modest proportions. These sections when fired would have to be mounted on a wall so it couldn't be over large in weight. As a rough estimate I concluded that the finished ammonite should be about two metres in diameter. The next task was to rough out some tentative designs to decide how many individual sections might be needed to make the finished sculpture, bearing in mind that the outer segments should be large enough to be illustrated with historical scenes. After several attempts the best design was that which had twenty two pieces in the outer layer all of which were of a reasonable size and format to decorate. Going back from this outer layer to the centre of the ammonite I estimated that over eighty individual sections would have to be made to complete the project. Having arrived at this preliminary number of segments, I started researching into the history of the county and came up with a list of over forty facets that might be used to illustrate the outer ones. These were put to members in a later newsletter to decide which to use. At this stage it was suggested that we might illustrate the segments of the second layer in to record the fossil record of the county and after more research I managed to come up with illustrations to support this idea. We didn't know at the time how important this record was to be, until the local coast was designated as a World Heritage Site and dubbed the Jurassic Coast.

With the research completed and the illustrations finally agreed, I made a life-size plan of the ammonite on a sheet of thick polythene the idea behind this being that it could be used as a guide for making each segment so that they locked perfectly into each other. Some discussions were then held about what clay should used for the project and how it should be glazed. It was decided that a grogged stoneware clay should be used as this would be less prone to warping and for the glaze I suggested that a manganese gold slip should be used as it looked very much like the iron pyrites that many of the local fossils were made of. A number of test pieces were then made and fired. These were very successful so a number of all day workshops were arranged at Upwey village hall where we had held many of our summer workshops. Apart from a few inner sections most segments had to be made individually. All of these had to be arched to give a three dimensional effect and as each segment was made from a flat rolled out sheet of clay calculations had to be made to allow for this. Allowances also had to be made for shrinkage in the firing and for what is known as clay memory. A number of fired clay templates were made to overcome the later but they weren't always successful. At the end of each workshop I took the finished segments home to make any last minute adjustments against the full scale plan, and they would then be dried and biscuit fired ready for the next workshop. After a while this arrangement became more unwieldy because of the size of the unfired segments, so it was agreed that future workshops would be held in my studio.

By this time we were becoming aware of the possible overall cost of the project. In addition to the material and firing costs money would have to be found for the erection of the ammonite and any publicity. A suitable wall to support it, preferably in an enclosed area to cut down the risk of it being vandalised, also had to be agreed. To help raise enough money to complete the project local people and businesses were invited to sponsor the decorated outer segments of the ammonite. A grant was sought from the West Dorset District Council towards the overall costs and jumble and car boot sales were held to make up any shortfall. All these efforts resulted in enough money being found to cover all our estimated costs. Only the wall needed to be found. This problem was discussed with the Arts Centre and they suggested that the tall red brick wall that formed the back boundary of their enclosed rear garden might be suitable provided that it would take the weight of the sculpture. Our Chairman, who worked for a large building firm before he became a professional potter, carried out a survey of this wall and decreed that it would take the weight. So, it was all systems go. More making workshops were arranged at the cottage. By now each segment being made and decorated was getting quite large so it wasn't possible to lay the finished pieces out in my workshop. The only suitable area to do this was in our dining room so before every workshop I had to put furniture to one side and lay out the polythene sheet, which had a full scale plan of the ammonite drawn on it, on the dining room carpet. I would lay out the finished segments on the plan and semi dry curved sheets of clay would then be cut so that they formed the next few segments to be decorated. Once decorated they would be left to dry out so that they could be biscuit fired. At the end of each workshop I would collect all the segments and put the glazed ones in boxes in our garage together with the floor plan. The others would be moved to the workshop so that I could glaze and fire them before the next workshop.

Overall the making and glazing of the ammonite took over eighteen months. It was finished just before one of our autumn exhibitions at Bridport Arts Centre and it was laid out in pride of place in the centre of the Allsop Gallery. Early in the following year our Chairman, using his old building skills, started to erect the ammonite on the wall in the garden at the back of the Arts Centre. Any gaps between the segments were filled in with a dark brown grout which fitted in well with the overall gold finish. Once up it was photographed from various angles so that the best viewpoint could be reproduced as a postcard. A framed list showing who sponsored a particular segment was displayed near the entrance to the garden together with details of who decorated it. All that remained was to get a local dignitary to officially unveil it. The local Mayor agreed to do this. Quite a crowd, including sponsors and group members, turned up for the ceremony which got a good write-up in the local press. The project had involved a lot of effort to complete but in the end it seemed well worth it.

The Bridport Ammonite

31. HAYMAKING AND OTHER TASKS

Throughout the year there are a lot of jobs that have to be done by farmers to keep their land in good order, and to ensure that there is sufficient food for their animals during the winter. These include haymaking, hedge cutting and manuring. These tasks have been carried out for centuries and before the introduction of machinery were very labour intensive and also very much a part of the social life of the countryside. Thomas Hardy gives some splendid examples of this in his novels. Nowadays things are very different and with modern machinery one person can do the work of many, but it can be a very solitary and lonely job however when compared with the camaraderie of earlier days.

The work still has to be mainly carried out during the daylight hours, and when it is dry, so the summer months tend to be the busiest and hay making is usually done in July. The tall grass in the meadows is cut mechanically and left to dry and every other day or so it is turned mechanically to assist this process, then when dry it is collected and bundled up by another machine. These days for the most part the bundles of hay are huge cylindrical affairs often wrapped in black plastic sheeting. Some bales however are still the traditional oblong cube affairs and they are often sold in this format. Many farmers now give their meadows an earlier cut in late spring if it is growing strongly, this is then fermented to make silage, a pleasant smelling nutritious winter feed, that can be used in place of hay. All this activity means that the village is a fairly noisy place during the summer months, with large tractors and trailers going up and down the lanes for most of the day.

Hedges are often cut in the winter as they cannot be cut in spring and summer until after the birds have finished nesting. A single mechanical hedge cutter can trim a lot of hedgerows in a few days but it doesn't collect the trimmings up however; these are left in the lanes where they are gradually broken down by passing traffic. Lane verges are usually trimmed back in July when many wild flowers have seeded and the caterpillars of early spring butterflies that feed on them have pupated. Some verges however are not trimmed because they are particularly rich in wild flowers or have rare species growing on them, and these are marked with   blue posts at the beginning and end of such areas.

Manuring can be done at any time of the year. A mechanical muck spreader can distribute manure in the form of solid particles of well rotted straw and animal dung, or in a liquid form. The latter is called 'slurry' which is prepared in a pit from animal dung and urine. It smells much stronger than the solid manure and, if you are in a car passing a field that has had slurry spread on it you will need to close all the windows. It really does smell foul!

An Old Hay Turning Machine

32. DORSET BIRDS

For most of my life I have had an interest in birds and this interest has waxed and waned over the years. Sometimes it was very strong and I would go on holiday with a friend to remote parts of Wales and Scotland to photograph seabirds. At other times it meant just feeding a few birds in the garden. I never considered myself a 'twitcher' who would chase after a rarity that could be added to a list of birds seen.

For some months before the move my interest in bird life was at a low ebb, but this quickly changed after our arrival in Dorset because whilst I was working on the outside of the cottage I spotted four buzzards wheeling overhead in the thermals created by the August heat. They were large magnificent birds who reminded me of the condors that had recently been featured in a television series about the fauna of South America. I had not seen so many buzzards in the wild before and this experience quickly rekindled my interest in birds again. Soon afterwards I became a member of the Dorset Trust for Nature Conservation (DTNC) and the Royal Society for the Protection of Birds (RSPB). Both these charities had reservations in Dorset where many species of birds might be seen. The country around the village also attracted a lot of birds, including some species that I had not previously seen.

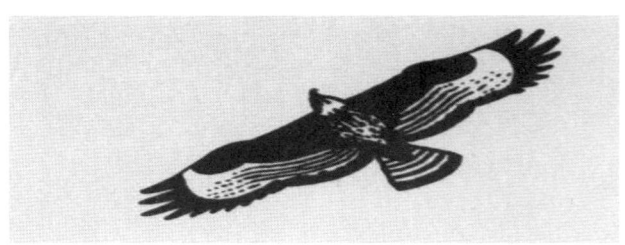

One of the places I frequently went to watch birds was Radipole Lake in Weymouth, a big reed edged lake run by the RSPB in the centre of the town which contains a large thatched nature centre and a good number of hides. There are several sign posted trails running through the reed beds which enable viewers to watch many of the birds that inhabit the reservation, including reed warblers, sedge warblers and the rare cettis warbler together with the bearded tit. The nature centre has several telescopes to give a close-up of some of the rarities that put in an appearance from time to time and a daily list of birds seen is put on display. The most fabulous bird I saw there was a Spoonbill, which adopted a pose reminiscent of an Audubon bird illustration, and evidently stayed for several days. The RSPB have another reservation nearby at Lodmoor which is also a reeded area that provides a home for several warblers. Its main attraction however is the bitterns that have recently been seen there and it is hoped that they will soon start a breeding colony.

A Bittern in the Reeds

The Isle of Portland is also an interesting place for bird watching and Portland Bill at the southern tip of this promontory provides a first landfall for many of the migratory birds that come here in the summer. The lighthouse there is often festooned with all kinds of warblers in early spring together with various members of the swallow family. Another good place for seeing birds in Dorset is Brownsea Island near Poole where the DTNC run a reservation and organise trips to see a number of species of terns including Sandwich Terns. This island is also a place where Red Squirrels still exist together with a number of rare bats.

Hardown Hill which overlooks our village is also a habitat for a number of unusual birds. Since coming here I have spotted Dartford Warblers there together with Nightjars, Yellow Hammers and Snipe. Some common birds seem to have diminished in numbers since I came to Whitchurch. Song Thrushes. Sparrows and Starlings however, whose numbers have diminished elsewhere, appear to be holding their own but sadly some birds such as the Skylark and the Lapwing have completely disappeared.

Birds have been the subject of many of my monthly Nature Notes. In fact I have probably referred to them more often than any other fauna and flora, including butterflies, as they do seem to hold a special attraction for many of my readers. Long may they continue to do so.

A Dartford Warbler

33. THE MORWIT PLAYERS

Shortly after I became a member of the Village Hall Committee a suggestion was made that perhaps we could put on some amateur theatricals as a way of raising more funds. Some years before there had been a local amateur group called the Morwhit Players that had put on shows at the Village Hall but it had been disbanded. Feelers were put out to some of the old players who still lived locally to see whether they would be prepared to act with a resurrected group and new blood was also sought at the same time. The responses were very encouraging and soon we had a fair number of people who were prepared to act in productions and others who could help in other ways e.g. with lighting, props, music, programmes, prompting, make-up, wardrobe, publicity and box office. So a new theatrical group came into being which at first decided that they would be called 'The New Morwit Players' but later they adopted the title of the original players. Among the people who put their names forward to help were Doreen, who said that she would like to act, and myself who volunteered to help back- stage.

The stage in the hall faced the centre section of the audience seating and could be drawn out to double its size. It had heavy curtains that could be opened and closed by draw strings from a side lobby which also contained a very basic lighting control board. Lighting presented some difficulties however because the stage could only be well lit by two very ancient spotlights which were seldom used because the replacement bulbs were prohibitively expensive. I mentioned this in the Five Bells one evening and a local car mechanic suggested that it might be possible to provide footlights, stage-lights and spotlights by using old car headlights run off 12 volt car batteries. The Morwhits agreed that we should try this and so the car mechanic and I spent a few evenings setting them up. The results were not all that good but on balance seemed better than using the old spotlights.

While the lighting was under consideration rehearsals were started for two plays entitled 'A Friend for Alice' and 'George' which would be presented on the same evening. Volunteers came forward to help with Props, Make-up, Wardrobe, Prompting, Publicity and Box Office and I agreed to help out wherever possible. The production was a great success and was followed later in the year by a Christmas Concert entitled 'Around the World in Eighty Daze' Doreen enjoyed being in these first productions and for her it was the beginning of a successful acting career with the Morwhits which lasted for a good number of years. I kept giving a hand back-stage whenever necessary.

Every year the Morwhits produced a new play or plays and also put on an evening of village entertainments. Each time the performances improved in quality and the lighting also got much better when a new landlord at the Five Bells, who had previously been a TV lighting technician, joined the group. He managed to secure some more up to date spotlights and also made improvements to the lighting control board. A new Director, with previous experience in producing plays, joined the players and was able to tackle more difficult productions. These included 'Murdered to Death' by Peter Gordon, 'A Civil Marriage' by Richard Tanitch, 'My Wife's Family' by Fred Duprez, 'Surprise Package' and 'Lets Be Friends' by Cherry Voight. One play called 'Where the Devil Bertie Is' was written by the Director's son. This was a play with a difference, one specially created for the Group's zany talents. Local artists produced some splendid designs for posters and programme illustrations to accompany these productions and the local press wrote some stunning reviews. Several productions were also recorded on video-tape and camera.

Taking part in these productions was great fun and raised a lot of money for the upkeep of the village hall. It was hard work on occasions but there was a lot of camaraderie amongst those taking part in them and also a sense of fulfilment. Like many enterprises however the players run out of steam and sadly The New Morwits went the way of the original group. Perhaps the next generation will revive them!

A Morwhit's Programme Cover by Kate Hill

34. ENTERTAINING

Trumps In makes a very good venue for entertaining friends and acquaintances. In summer parties are held, weather permitting, in the patio or on the lawn at the back of the cottage, and in winter in the cottage itself. Both of us love entertaining and try to do so as often as possible.

In the early days it was difficult because we couldn't afford to provide much in the way of food and drink. Shortly after the move however, I discovered a shop in Bridport that sold many kinds of concentrated grape juice, e.g. Merlot, Temperillo, Riesling, Chardonnay etc., that could be fermented at home and in a few weeks end up as a very drinkable wine. It wasn't very long before I had amassed several five gallon barrels of both red and white wine. Then a local furniture maker let me have some oak shavings which I put into some of the barrels of red wine to give an authentic cask finish. Friends seemed to enjoy them and for some time they became the mainstay of our hospitality.

Some of our parties were often arranged to celebrate certain events such as special birthdays or reaching a pensionable age. Others would host an annual event such as flying kites in the field next door which took place for a number of years following an international kite festival in Weymouth. Yet others were after a Dorset Pottery Group workshop or kiln firing event. In some cases they were convened on the spur of the moment. A major eclipse of the sun also provided an excuse for a party although on that occasion the day turned out to be very cloudy. The number of people invited varied but could be up to 30 plus. The food we provided was mostly home cooked and often home grown when I had the allotment. Then there were more formal occasions where we returned invitations to dinner parties and 'drinks and nibbles'.

All of these occasions made for a great deal of social interaction and a network of friends which is so important in a rural community.

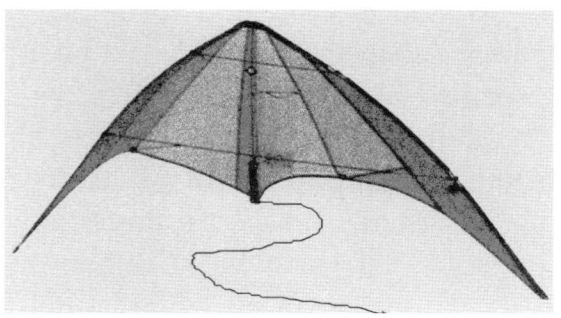

One of our Kites

35. USING COMPUTERS

After coming to Dorset I became involved in writing numerous articles on various subjects, producing posters, issuing press releases and publishing newsletters. At first I managed this by using a manual typewriter and a photocopier, but later I moved on to an electric typewriter and then a basic word processing machine. All these methods had limitations however and I became more and more interested in the possibility of acquiring a home computer to assist me with this work.

Before the move I had some experience of using a personal computer at work. This was an Apple computer called 'Lisa' that used an early black and white windows system. I got on with this machine quite well using it mainly for word processing and statistical illustrations. The prospect of buying and utilising a modern PC therefore was not as daunting as it might have been for someone who had had no previous experience of using such a machine. After doing some research into what was available and what it would cost, I decided to contact a local firm to see what they could offer rather than going to one of the larger suppliers. It seemed at the time that I might get a better follow up service from a supplier if he was based nearby. This was particularly important to me as I was suffering from a hearing problem, and would prefer to sort out any difficulties on a face to face basis rather than over the telephone. After getting several quotes I finally purchased an up to date PC and a printer from a firm in Axminster which came with Windows 98 and a lot of other software. Shortly afterwards I obtained a scanner that had the facility to scan transparencies as well as printed photographs, the former being the format of many of my earlier pictures.

The whole set-up was magic to use. On the word processing side there were hundreds of typefaces and sizes that could be utilised. Visually I was able to convert photographs to all kinds of artistic prints and these could be saved on the hard disk with back up copies that could be made on a CD. They other main facilities available were the ability to search the Internet for information and to contact people by E-mail.

The ability to use a computer is probably the most important skill that one should have at the present time. I have probably been much slower to acquire this ability than a younger person but I have persevered however, and now feel quite competent with the technology. Doreen feels the same as me and she now has her own laptop and Internet connection. It seems essential in a rural area to be able to have a lot of things delivered and also to be in touch with friends. The computer is an indispensable tool for doing this. It is also essential to have contact with a local expert who can quickly come to sort out any computer problems that might arise. We have been very lucky in this respect by discovering a true expert in the village.

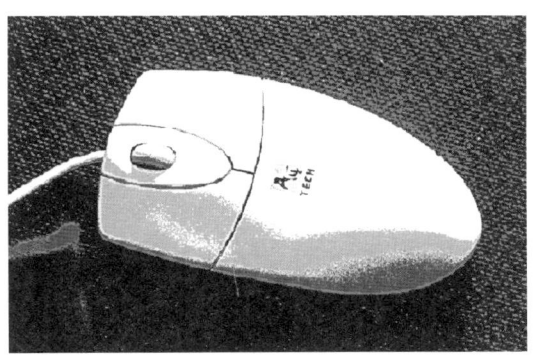

My Trusty Mouse

APPENDIX I

A Selection of Articles Written for

Dorset Pottery Group Newsletters

MACPHERSON'S ROD

Throw, wedge, pug. These are all well known potter's terms and will be understood by anyone who has had but a brief contact with the craft. Other terms are more personal and arise from a function within a group or even from one's own individual method of working.

For example, some years ago when I first became interested in pottery I set up a small workshop with some friends In Blackheath. Prepared clay was very expensive so it was decided that we would prepare our own. Barrels were bought and an absorbent trough was built in the garden. The search for clay was on. It was discovered at Aylesford in Kent and consisted of large chunks of hard gritty material from which we hoped to obtain a smooth throwing body. The main problem was how to remove the grit We tried breaking the clay down in the barrels, then adding water and when the clay was liquid sieving it through a 20 mesh, a 40 mesh and finally through a 60 mesh sieve. This was a very laborious process so finally, to save time, we placed the three sieves, which were of rectangular shape, one upon the other and poured the liquid clay into the uppermost one. It passed through the 20 mesh without trouble, also the 40 mesh, but when it came to the 60 mesh there was a bottleneck. How could we overcome this problem?

There was a member of the group who, although not actively a potter, was very interested in what we were doing. He devised a system of old hair and clothes brushes which covered the width of the 60 mesh sieve and when connected to a dowel, which passed out of the end of the sieve, could be moved to cover the whole length of it as well. A few strokes of the dowel and the clay was through. Fred Macpherson had solved the problem and in his honour we called the brush device 'Macpherson 's Rod'.

GRATITUDE TO TEACHERS

How often, when one sees or hears a programme about a person's life, is gratitude expressed to a particular teacher who has had a great influence on their development. Many members will possibly remember teachers who have enriched their lives.

As far as pottery is concerned I met my most influential and greatly loved teacher quite by accident. My chosen profession had been electrical engineering but after completing National Service I decided that I would like to take up a craft. The local evening classes for pottery were full so it was suggested that I contacted the Woolwich Polytechnic,which was a 5 miles bus journey away from where I was then living, to see whether they had any vacancies. I was already familiar with the Poly because I had previously been a full time engineering student there. I didn't however, know the Head of the Art Department who also took the evening pottery classes. His name was Heber Matthews. He said that there were vacancies and I was able to sign up for three evenings a week.

My first lessons were about how to knead clay and how to centre it on the wheel. From there I went on to throwing simple cylinders. My first efforts were hopeless! I wasn't a natural and I thought of giving it all up. Heber Matthews was very patient with me at this stage and with his encouragement my throwing gradually improved. He also taught me how to turn pots to form good foot rings, how to pull handles and to form spouts. He talked about the aesthetic qualities of pottery and what made a good pot. At the same time he started introducing me to the history of pottery and the Artist Potters' movement in the UK. All this really fired my imagination and set me on a lifelong interest in pottery. Thanks to him I was really hooked!

He was very modest about his part in the Artist Potters' movement and it was only later that I found out that he was a foremost student of William Staite Murray and had taught Hans Coper how to throw. He was pottery consultant to the Rural Industries Bureau for some years and a founder member of the Crafts Centre of Great Britain. On the practical side he was a wonderful thrower and he developed some

splendid earthernware glazes that had the quality of oriental stoneware. His own work was not prolific but what he did create was highly individual and reflected a fine artist working from within. A number of his pots are in the V & A collection.

Above all he was a warm patient man with a quiet sense of humour, taking delight in the small things of life and in the passing show, penetrating but never bitter.

Heber Matthews died in 1959 at the tragic early age of 53. His spirit however is always with me. Whenever I look at a new pot that I have made I always ask myself this question. *Would Heber have approved of this?* It was a great priviledge and honour to have known him.

Alan Ashpool

Heber Matthews, A.R.C.A.

MAKING POTS IN THE FIFTIES

THEN AND NOW
A PERSONAI VIEW

When I started potting in the Fifties the atmosphere was very different to that of today. There were no Groups or Associations that one could join. Pottery was taught at Evening Classes but instruction was only given in a limited number of techniques with one or two well tried bodies and a couple of glazes. There was very little room for experiment. Everything seemed secretive and constrained. Pots were mostly 'in the round' usually thrown, although some were made by coiling or in press moulds. Firings were carried out in gas or electric kilns all of a non-portable construction.

There were not many books available about making pottery especially any with a range of glaze and body recipes. Bernard Leach's 'A Potters Book ' was widely used. There was a useful Foyle's handbook about pottery by Murray Fieldhouse and also 'The Pottery Book' by the Val Bakers but that was about all. Some contact with other potters and their ideas could be made through 'Pottery Quarterly' magazine. But again not a lot of technical help was forthcoming. More information however, was available about English studio potters and the history of pottery. These included George Winglield Digby's excellent 'Book of English Potters' and Muriel Rose's 'Artist Potters in England'. Worldwide history was very well covered in the Faber monographs on pottery and porcelain edited by W B. Honey. These all approached pottery from the aesthetic rather than the technical viewpoint.

Interest in pottery, especially stoneware, had become a vogue in England before the second world war and potters such as Bernard Leach, William Staite Murray, and Michael Cardew had produced work which was greatly to influence the direction the first generation of post war potters took. There was great interest in early far eastern pottery particularly Chinese work of the Tang and Sung dynasties, Medieval English jugs and slipware were also a strong influence. A great pot, , whether it was ancient or modern, was thought to be one that made an aesthetic statement by itself quite independently of the person who made it.

How different things are today. There are a great number of books available which give in depth technical information about all aspects of pottery making. Experimentation and diversity are encouraged and there is a ready exchange of information. Many more ways of firing are available and the spectrum of colours widened at all temperatures. Pottery Groups have sprung up all over the country in which members provide help for each other. More and more potters are making their own personal statements through their work rather than using aesthetic statements from an earlier age.

Editor

SOME THOUGHTS ABOUT POTTERY............

THOUGHTS ABOUT CLAY.....Surely the potter's staff of life. What wonderful material it is. Weathered from ancient rocks its very plastic nature lends itself to a multitude of working methods. Yet, when subjected to the heat of the potter's kiln it assumes the hardness and durability of the rocks from whence it came, and the plastic image is frozen in time. What magic!

THOUGHTS ABOUT THROWING.....A pot as it is being thrown can be likened to a blossoming flower. The centred clay a bud. A plunge of the thumb and the bud has opened. Upwards and outwards spontaneously, like a filmed sequence of a growing plant that has been taken on a time lapse camera. Thrusting! Alive!

THOUGHTS ABOUT BOWLS.....Probably the earliest pottery forms to be created. Surely these are the most widely used and versatile of pots. At their simplest they can be used for cooking and serving food. Alternatively, soaring up from their narrow base they, unlike any other form, can lend themselves to a wide variety of decoration both inside and out. What diversity! What opportunity!

THOUGHTS ABOUT JUGS.....No pots have more feeling about them than jugs. What generous things they are. And what perfect forms. Pots that are giving in function rather than taking, social rather than individual, yet full of character. These qualities are perhaps most evident in our own splendid English medieval jugs!

THOUGHTS ABOUT GLAZES.....What experiences a glaze can recall. Those sensuous joys of childhood. The lustrous depths of glass marbles. Pebbles. Seashells. The excitement on first seeing a clutch of thrushes' eggs so blue and silky against the mud lining of the nest. Are these the true delights behind our more sophisticated appreciations?

THOUGHTS ABOUT SHARDS.....Shards. Those bones of pots gone by. Those jewels of history and the imagination. How many stories could they tell. Hold a fragment of the sensitively thrown rim of a Roman cooking pot and you have bridged the centuries. Discover a piece of an old salt glazed pot and imagine the whole. What an adventure!

Alan Ashpool

NEW POTS FOR OLD?

During the last three or four decades there has been much progress in the field of studio pottery. Many new techniques have been introduced, e.g. the use of laminated and paper clays. There has been the adoption of pottery making methods previously confined to industry, such as slip casting and extrusion. New ways of firing have been introduced including pit firings and newspaper kilns. Decoration now encompasses such things as the use of print and the fixation of smoke patterns formed by the actual firing. Many colour pigments have been introduced which can be fired to much higher temperatures than before. All these advances have resulted in the United Kingdom having today one of the richest diversity of pottery and pottery makers in the world. Have we, however, lost anything on the way?

It is perhaps too early to say definitely whether anything has been lost, but there seem to be several trends which are disquieting. There is for example a growing tendency by some modern potters to refer disparagingly to pots being made by traditional methods as 'Brown Pots' and of no interest. Decoration seems to have become the most important aspect of a pot rather than a harmonious combination of form, decoration, glaze and fired body. Past influential potters are constantly being set up as 'Aunt Sallys' and criticised for the influence they have had on pottery making. A lot of galleries now appear to show only the work of fashionable established potters. There seems to be a widening gap between Arts and Crafts. The wonderful term 'Potter' is increasingly being supplanted by 'Ceramicist'. Some of the pots now being made seem to lack the *'Tingle Factor'* that could be experienced from looking at and handling pots made in the past.

Some members may feel differently about these trends and it would be interesting to hear their views. Any contribution would be welcomed and published in the next Newsletter.

Alan Ashpool

APPENDIX 2

A Table Showing Butterflies
Likely To Be Seen In The Marshwood Vale

SPECIES TO BE SEEN	BEST TIME	BEST LOCATIONS
Small Skipper	July	Meadows and Hedgerows
Large Skipper	June/July	Meadows and Lane Verges
Clouded Yellow	August *	Meadows near Prime Coppice
Brimstone	April and August	Lane Verges and Clearings
Green-veined White	May and August	Hedgerows and Gardens
Orange Tip	May	Where Garlic Mustard Flowers
Green Hairstreak	May	Amongst Gorse on Hardown Hill
Small Copper	August	Meadows and Hedgerows
Common Blue	June and August	Hedgerows and Gardens
Holly Blue	May and August	Meadows and Gardens
Red Admiral	August/September	Orchards and Gardens
Painted Lady	August *	Bramble Hedgerows
Small Tortoiseshell	June to September	Gardens and Hedgerows
Peacock	April and August	Gardens and Meadows
Comma	April and July	Gardens and Hedgerows
Small Pearl-bordered Fritillary	June	Hardown Hill
Silver-washed Fritillary	July and August	Coppices
Speckled Wood	June and September	Shady Lanes
Wall	May and August	Hardown Hill
Marbled White	July/August	Meadows around Prime Coppices
Grayling	July/August	Hardown Hill
Gatekeeper	July/August	Meadows and Lanes
Meadow Brown	July/August	Meadows and Lanes
Small Heath	June	Hardown Hill
Ringlet	July	Meadows Around Prime Coppices
	* Not Every Year	

APPENDIX 3

A Selection of Nature Notes

NATURE NOTES

By the time these Nature Notes are published I will have completed and returned this year's Garden Butterflies Count survey form to Butterfly Conservation. This survey covers the period from the beginning of April until the end of October and includes 22 species of butterflies and 4 moths that might be seen in the garden. Like last year the survey form asks for details about your garden such as size, locality, what flowers it contains that provide nectar and what food-plants for caterpillars. The results will be published early next year.

What a fantastic summer this has been for sighting different species of butterflies and moths. The very hot weather resulted in many more species and numbers than usual migrating from Southern Europe. In particular large numbers of *Painted Lady* butterflies arrived in June from North Africa and have had a very successful breeding season in Dorset. Vast numbers of *Silver Y* moths also arrived from the South and were seen feeding on nectar plants during the day. The real gems to be seen were the *Jersey Tiger Moth*. Quite a few were spotted in Bridport and in the Marshwood Vale. I was lucky enough to spot and photograph one in my garden! This moth sometimes turns up in South Devon but is rarely seen here. Other unusual migrant butterflies to have been spotted on the south coast include *Long-tailed Blues* and *Swallowtails*. The warm weather also resulted in the spotting of additional numbers of some of our resident butterflies e.g. *White-letter Hairstreaks* in Bradpole and *Adonis Blues* on Portland

This year has also been good for Hawk-moths. On the Garden Butterfly Count survey form I was able to record sightings of *Humming-bird Hawk-moths* in July, August and September. This Summer visitor is rarely seen in most years and this year's numbers must be the result of the very hot weather in Southern Europe. During August I received telephone calls about the sighting of a *Convolvulus Hawk-moth* and an *Oleander Hawk-moth*. Again the sightings of these rare migrant moths could probably be put down to the same hot weather. Towards the end of August a lady came to the cottage with a full grown caterpillar of a Death's head Hawk-moth which she had found feeding on her potato plants. These particular moths are regular rare migrants to the UK in the Spring and often raise a brood here. It was the first time however that I had seen a full grown caterpillar of the species. It was very exciting.

Alan Ashpool, Trumps In Cottage

NATURE NOTES

In previous Nature Notes I have written about fungi and when and where they might be seen in this area. Details of both edible and poisonous varieties were given. All those I described had English names such as *Wood Blewit, Fly Agaric, Giant Puffball, Shaggy Inkcap* and *Chicken of the Woods*. However in fact only about a hundred of the thousand commoner species found in this country have such English titles and the rest have long scientific names in Latin. All this is to change however. In an attempt to make fungi more accessible to non-specialists, and foster more interest in them English Nature, Scottish Natural Heritage and the wildflower charity Plantlife International, have joined forces with the British Mycological Society to produce a list of acceptable English names for the rest of these commoner species. The names were drawn up by Elizabeth Holden, a Scottish based mycologist, using a combination of old and new guides to fungi and also her imagination. So fungi known by the Latin name of *Bisporella citrina* are now called **Lemon Disco**, *Bjerkandera adjusta* are now **Smokey Brackets**, *Cudonia confusa* is **Cinnamon Jellybaby**, *Verpa conica* are **Thimble Morel**, *Hyphodontia sambuci* are **Elder Whitewash** and *Phellodon niger* are **Black Tooth**. These names seem very apt and I look forward to them being used in any new guides about our native species.

Fungi, which can also be called mushrooms or toadstalls, are unique in that they cannot really be referred to as flora. None of them contain the green pigment chlorophyll so they cannot make their own food by the process known as photosynthesis. None are green in the sense that a tree or flowering plant is. They get their nourishment from dead organisms, excrement, dead vegetation etc or by being parasites on living plants and trees. Mushrooms are normally defined as the edible, spore-producing bodies of some edible fungi. The term toadstool on the other hand is applied to the spore-producing bodies of fungi that are not only inedible but may also be highly dangerous.

One way to observe how quickly these fruiting bodies appear is to grow field mushrooms at home. Kits for growing them are available from Garden Centres and Seed Merchants. It is quite magical to see how quickly the fruiting bodies swell from pinhead size to large flat headed specimens. Last year I obtained from Dobies Seeds wooden plugs which contained the spores of *Oyster Mushrooms* and *Shitaki Mushrooms*. These were placed in holes drilled in freshly cut logs. The logs were first placed in black sacks for four months and then planted out in the garden according to Dobies' instructions. These logs should now produce mushrooms several times a year for up to five years. At the time of writing I have had a large number of Oyster Mushrooms growing. Shitaki mushrooms however take longer and, fingers crossed, should start producing next Spring.

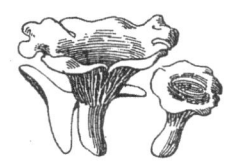

Alan Ashpool,

Trumps In Cottage

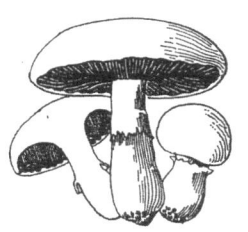

NATURE NOTES

Last month I mentioned that most birds would soon stop singing and would probably not be heard again until early next Spring. In particular I mentioned how much the song of the wonderful Blackbird would be missed.

Whilst I was on holiday in Majorca in June the local English Newspaper ran an article entitled ' The Morning Chorus'. It started with a question about what musical instrument unites Beethoven, Tchaikovsky, Scott Joplin and Louis Armstrong. The answer given was ' the Blackbird's song'. This verdict was the result of information given in a number of readers letters to the Editor of the Newspaper.

It all began evidently when someone from Essex wrote to say that a Blackbird in his garden regularly sang a ' charming, four-note phrase in A major' and enquired whether other readers had similarly talented birds in their gardens. They certainly had!

One recalled a cock Blackbird which sang alternatively the first and second phrase of Scot Joplins ' The Entertainer'. Another claimed that for a decade a series of Blackbirds in his garden had sung the two opening bars of Beethoven's Violin Concerto. What next? A third reader said that in his garden he had heard phrases from Louis Armstrong's solos and snatches from Bix Beiderbecke's ' Singing The Blues'. Another bird preferred the first three bars of the wartime song ' The Last Time I Saw Paris'. There were many other examples quoted including one reader who had identified the charming, four- note phrase in A Major mentioned in the first letter as the opening from Tchaikovsky's 'Eugen Onegin'.

It would be interesting to hear whether any readers of these Nature Notes have identified any other melodies being sung by local Blackbirds.

Another interesting thing that I have read lately about bird song is about some birds, especially Starlings, mimicking the many different ringing tones of mobile phones. This is evidently most prevalent in towns. Lets hope that it does not catch on here!

Alan Ashpool, Trumps In Cottage.

NATURE NOTES

Many of our native amphibians will have started breeding by now. All of them lay their eggs in water. Most readers will be familiar with the mass of spawn and tadpoles of the common frog in local ponds. Some may even remember from their childhood days keeping some spawn in old jam jars, watching the tadpoles hatch and then growing legs before turning into miniature frogs.

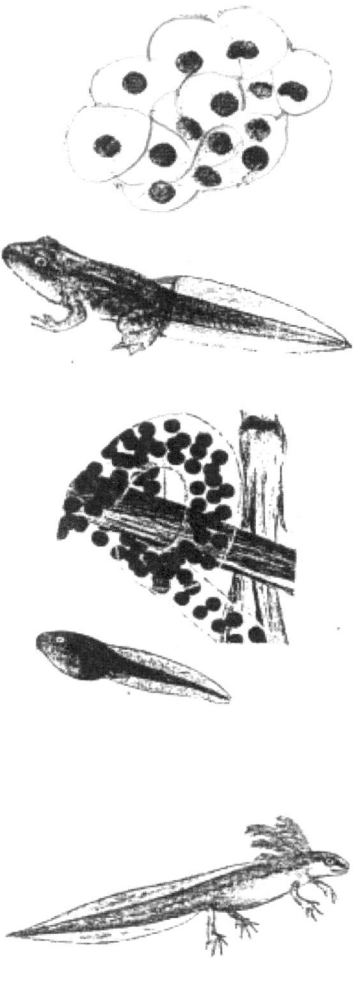

Other amphibians produce their eggs differently. Toads lay them in a long string which is wound around plants and twigs in the water. Newts on the other hand lay their eggs singly often wrapped in the leaf of a water plant. Toad spawn hatches into tadpoles which are similar to, but smaller than, frog tadpoles. Toad tadpoles grow legs in the same way as frogs before they finally change into small adults. Young newts are entirely different. When they hatch they already have legs and look like miniature adults with the addition of frothy gills each side of the head.

The tadpoles of both frogs and toads feed on vegetable matter until they turn into adults. Baby newts however are carnivorous from the start feeding on such things as water fleas and small worms. Frog tadpoles are often eaten by fish, the larger newts and dragonfly larvae. Toad tadpoles seem to be protected from this fate by a bitter poisonous substance which also protects them in adult life. A heron or a cat will readily eat a frog but will soon drop a toad! Newt larvae have few enemies except perhaps other newts.

In this area I have only seen *common frogs*, *common toads* and *palmate newts*. I have been told however that *smooth newts* and the rare protected *crested newts* do appear in some of the larger ponds and lakes in the Marshwood Vale. Only frogs spawn in my garden pond together with the small *palmate newts*. *Toads* prefer deeper water. There are no fish in my pond and, as *palmate newts* don't eat tadpoles, I am able to rear a good number of *frogs* each year.

I hope that this state of affairs will continue but I am perturbed by recent news about a virus that is killing Britain's frogs. This is said to be worse than myxomatosis, the plague that destroyed the rabbit population 40 years ago. The virus causes the frogs feet to drop off. It takes a considerable for the animals to die and there are indications that their numbers are permanently depressed in some areas. Lets hope that it passes this area by! Fortunately it does not seem to infect toads and newts.

Alan Ashpool
Trumps In Cottage.

NATURE NOTES

Now that their leaves have fallen this is a good time to look at the silhouettes of our wonderful native deciduous trees. Each one has a distinctive outline.

In the Marshwood Vale the magnificent *Oak* predominates. It is broad and stocky. How well it has served us over the years. Not for nothing is it sometimes referred to as the King of trees. There are also a large number of *Ash, Beech* and *Sycamore*s. The *Ash* which is said to have been named after the colour of its bark, is tall and slender. Its branches more evenly spaced than those of the Oak. The branches of the *Beech* are also evenly spaced and soar to a great height. When their leaves fall they retain their brilliant colouring for a long time which contrasts brilliantly with the smooth grey bark. The *Beech* is a painters tree and often features in Autumn landscapes. The branches of the *Sycamore* are also fairly evenly spaced. The trunk is grey and a little scaly. Some authorities say that the true name of this tree is the *Great Maple*. In smaller numbers other large trees to be seen locally include the *Horse Chestnut*, the *Willow* and several *Poplars*. See how many you can identify without having their leaves to refer to!

There is a certain amount of Folklore about trees. For instance it is said that if in the Spring the *Ash* is in full leaf before the *Oak* we shall have a rainy Summer. If however the *Oak* is out first then the Summer will be fine. It is also said that the Willow is a symbol of grief for those who have been forsaken in love.

Alan Ashpool, Trumps In Cottage

Oak

Beech

Sycamore